ABOUT THE AUTHOR

Max Evans, who lives in Taos, New Mexico, is no phony westerner. His hobby, and favorite sport, is roping calves—and he has won considerable prize money in many southwestern contests—consistently tieing calves in from fourteen to eighteen seconds. He has been a real working cowboy, a trapper, a ranch owner and operator. And no sequin-shirted dude, of the drug store or Hollywood cowboy variety, could ever have managed to be a close friend and confidant of Long John Dunn. For John Dunn could spot the ersatz variety a mile away.

Like Dunn, Max Evans has followed the lure of the mining boom, though Evans has interested himself more directly in the minerals themselves, and less on taking the gains away from the miners by card and wheel, than did old John. He has ridden from prospector to mining promotor with the same ease he subdues a bronc in the ring. Among his other accomplishments he has served either as an official or on the board of directors of four important mining enterprises in northern New Mexico.

As if these accomplishments were not enough, he is known also as a skilled cowboy artist—and finally as a writer of great power, salty idiom, and humor that stems from his close experience with horses and men.

He has sold scores of stories and articles to national and regional magazines, and is author of "Southwest Wind," a book of western-flavored short stories that has won wide literary acclaim. "Long John Dunn of Taos" will add greatly to his acceptance and fame as an honest and sensitive chronicler of his time and environment.

At present he is at work on a serious novel. And, since whatever he does he does with the seriousness and intensity of a true champ, he'll probably rope up that novel cleanly, surely, and with timing and skill enough to satisfy the critics.

LONG JOHN DUNN OF TAOS

GREAT WEST AND INDIAN SERIES XV

Long John Dunn of Taos

by Max Evans

WESTERNLORE PRESS
Los Angeles 41, California . . . 1959

COPYRIGHT 1959 BY
WESTERNLORE PRESS

Library of Congress Catalog No. 59-10903

PRINTED IN THE UNITED STATES OF AMERICA BY WESTERNLORE PRESS

AN APOLOGY TO THE READER

THIS is not my story. I have put it down the best I know how—as near as I could to the way Long John Dunn actually told it to me.

He lived, in his ninety or more years, one of the most incredible lives of any of the old-time westerners. He was top-notch in everything he did. John was one of the best gun fighters, gamblers, bronc-riders, ropers, stage-coach drivers, trail-herd drivers, saloon-keepers, out-laws and, ironically, a hard-headed business man.

During such a long and varied career it was only natural that a few events took place that cannot be mentioned today.

In the early days a man made a friend through trial and hardship. These old-timers remain fanatically loyal to one another. John was no exception. So, it is understandable and even laudable that a few names are left out of this chronicle. They are left out so as to protect those who were outside the law and who are still living, and likewise, to protect their friends and relatives.

But as one old-time friend of John's said, "There's plenty here to please anybody, because old John lived enough lives for a dozen adventurous men." It is John's story and, because he wanted it that way, I hereby dedicate the story and life of Long John Dunn to . . . Mabel Dodge Lujan.

Taos, New Mexico.

MAX EVANS.

ILLUSTRATIONS

LONG JOHN DUNN OF TAOS

I

In Victoria, Texas, 1857, a baby was born. From the noise he made, it sounded more like a panther. Long John Dunn raised hell for a long time after, in one form or another. The half-breed midwife who delivered him made a prophetic remark. She said, "This boy will go places. I can tell by the way he yells." She proved to be one hundred percent right.

"My folks were farmers," said Long John some ninety years later. "The love of the soil was written all over them. We were trying to make a living on a little rolling dry-land, slow-starvation farm. The plantation owners had most of the bottom land in those days and it was next to impossible around Victoria for a family in our poor financial state to make more than a bare existence.

"It was not long before we starved out there. My father had heard of good farming land in Missouri. So, he loaded our few possessions on a wagon and took off for that state. It proved to be a bad move. We didn't raise enough to feed the horses and my father decided the climate was not right for his health.

"Before I was big enough to reach a stirrup leather standing on tiptoe, we were back in Comanche County, Texas, not too far from the town of Waco. Then the great and bloody war between the states lured my father into the Confederate army."

John had one brother younger than he, and a sister a year older. They managed fairly well on the little farm they had acquired there, but this did not last long. His mother was afraid the Indians would raid them. They had heard about raids and killings all the way up from San Saba in Sabine County. So, they moved into town.

John's mother went to work for a number of store owners, sewing any and everything they asked her to. The family still had a mighty rough time of it because the wages were low.

His father returned with the South's beaten armies and they were all reunited and content enough to fig-ure that maybe they would have a little more to eat and a new pair of shoes once in a while. The way it turned out though, it was just another mouth to feed. His father had been wounded and was no longer able to work. John, before he died, in the telling of his story, spoke of this period in his life with a hard glint in his bright old eyes, and with that characteristic horse-like whistle in his nose.

"I started setting snare traps for rabbits out in the edge of town. It helped. More people lived on rabbits in those days than are living on beans now. It was like an uncle of mine said—that uncle I was soon to work for—'I've got to where I'm so fast on foot I can catch most any rabbit. The ones I can't catch are so lean they're not fit to eat anyhow.' "

At this time the state of Texas had been caught in the painful middle of the Reconstruction Period. Cattle were all over the state—by the hundreds of thousands. There was no market except for a limited few. Fort Sumner in New Mexico bought a little cattle for the Indians, through an Indian Agency which had a contract with the government. A limited number were also purchased at Fort Collins, Colorado. This market was so small it did not make a dent in the faded economy of Texas. There simply was no money to be had. People were forced to hunt game and scratch a living from the soil as best they could.

There was, too, a constant menace from the warring Comanches, who were raiding all over that area, killing, pillaging and burning. That famous and historic group, the Texas Rangers, originally was recruited to combat this menace. Their deeds of courage are legend in the fight to win the west. They were soon known everywhere as fearless, and deadly fighters, and they were given a healthly respect by those outside the law. John, himself, was in later years to escape narrowly from this organization.

Texas greatly suffered from the internal troubles of the Reconstruction. The paternal government had little sympathy for the well-being of a state recently in arms against the Union. Gradually, however, a small trade in cattle sprang up in the North. Baxter Springs and Abilene, Kansas, were beginning to be mentioned as possible markets. Light drives had already been made to these points, with fair success.

Another reason for interest in this new Northern route was the absence of Indian trouble. It was only natural men should hope to reach market without an arrow in the heart and one's scalp removed for a Comanche warrior's belt.

Although the demand was generally unsatisfactory, the faith of the drivers never faltered. Ironically, a group of Yankee businessmen were responsible for this show of confidence. A railroad had been laid to Abilene, Kansas. Stock yards were built for the accommodation of shippers during the summer of 1867. A firm of shrewd farseeing Yankees made great pretensions of having established a market and a meeting place for buyers and sellers alike. The promoters of the scheme had a contract with the railroad whereby they were to receive a bonus on all cattle shipped from that point. Texas drivers were offered every inducement to make Abilene their destination in the future.

The unfriendliness of other states toward Texas cattle, caused by ravages of fever imparted by Southern livestock to domestic animals, had resulted in a quarantine being enforced against all stock from the South. Matters were in an unsettled condition and less than one per cent of Texas cattle had found an outside market during the year 1867. Though most ranchmen were hopeful, these were trying years for a young man with no money, no backing, and no education.

It is in this time that the character of John Dunn was being formed, and things that happened in his later years can be more readily understood with such realization.

John's father died suddenly from the internal injuries received during the war. The family couldn't afford a funeral, with undertakers, so it fell, as their necessity, to put him away themselves.

"I dug my father's grave," John soberly recalled, in the telling of his story, and as he dredged his memory backwards in time. "For hours at a stretch I worked, until my hands were solid blisters, and my back pained from the long strain. I tried to numb my mind to what I was doing, but as I dug deeper into the ground a feeling of grim determination settled over me. I was dead-set in some way I would elevate myself out of the poverty that forced me to dig my own father's grave, and help make his casket."

Of his boyhood, John spoke little. Necessity had forced him into manhood even as he had grown into a tall snotty-nosed, loose-jointed, skinny-shinned kid. A short time after the funeral John decided to go out in the country and work for his uncle—an uncle by marriage, John Matthews. He figured he could make it a lot easier on his mother, since his uncle was to pay him twelve and one half dollars a month.

The only outlet for cotton during the Civil War period had been at Matamoros, near the mouth of the Rio Grande. It was contraband, and it was a long, dangerous haul to get it there. After the war the market opened up in the southern seaports, and Texas was in the beginning of the great industry, but at the time John went to work for his uncle this was only starting.

The work was hard, John didn't mind so much, because they fed well. His uncle was trying out cotton farming for the first time, and he put John to plowing with a pair of half-broken mules.

Even in his old age John's face lighted up when he talked of horses or mules. He had a fondness for them. "I'll never forget one big black mule," he recollected. "When I'd go to hook the trace-chain to the single-tree he'd be watching me, and I'd be watching him. For if I ever dropped my eyes, he'd try to kick my britches off. He only connected once, and even though it numbed my teehinder for a week, I didn't mind so much. There was a reason why I didn't mind so much." John chuckled and whistled as he told it. "I tied him with a well-rope to a snubbing-post, and beat him over the head with a piece of log chain until I was completely give out. My uncle bragged on me for this— saying I sure knew how to handle a mule.

"The beating didn't seem to bother the long-eared critter much, and I can swear he did the best day's work that day he'd ever done. You can treat almost any animal with kindness and get some results. Try this on a mule, and he'll kick your brains right out your ears."

More of John's story came out of these recollections. "My uncle was married to one of the fattest women I ever saw in my life," he declared. "She must have weighed as much as a yearling steer. But how that woman could cook! I ate like a starved wolf at her table. And I grew over three inches, straight up, while staying there.

"My uncle swore his wife got that fat from eating her own cooking. That might be the truth, because she sure did stash it away. She reminded me of a big old hog I slopped twice a day. Funny thing about that woman, though, she never did go outside—at least I never saw her if she did. My uncle said she couldn't get through the door. But I believe she could—or how in hell did she ever get in the house in the first place?

"Another different thing about her was that this big woman had no kids. In those days nearly every family had from two to twenty. One day I asked her about this, and she laughed, shaking all over. She said she was barren. I didn't know what she meant then, but later I heard a couple of ranchers talking about barren mares, and I understood.

"One afternoon while I was slopping the old sow, seven or eight Comanche Indians made a run across a little pasture where my uncle had several horses he was breaking. I yelled as loud as I could, dropped the slop-bucket, and ran for the house. My uncle came out to meet me and handed me a gun. I didn't know what kind of a gun it was, I just threw it up and pulled the trigger! Uncle hadn't fired a shot yet. He ran out into the pasture, screaming and cursing at the top of his voice. The Indians took off without any horses—except the ones they were riding.

"I followed my uncle toward the two Indians. One of them was dead. He'd been hit in the neck, and the other was rolling over and over, moaning and slobbering at the mouth like a mad dog. There was blood running from one of his ears, but I never did get to see where he was hit, because my uncle shot him again, and led me away.

"Next morning my uncle got up and dragged the two Indians off into a brushy gully. For a long time I could see buzzards circling, and knew they were having a feast.

"I remember that it was hotter than the mildews of hell that summer, and sometimes I really wanted to pull out. But my uncle said if they made a good crop, he'd give me fifteen dollars a month. I figured I could keep five each month, and send the rest to my ma."

One summer day, John was thinning cotton with a heavy iron hoe when one of his uncle's neighbors rode up, riding a keen looking bay stallion. His name was Dunchee and he had that look and feel that John's uncle had: that thin-hipped, brush-country look of being filed down by weather and trouble, until all that remained of the man was his long-handled moustache and sharp blue eyes and the prominent Adam's apple that bobbed when he spat tobacco juice at the dry earth.

"Name's Dunchee," he said. "Heard you're a pretty good hand."

"I shore as hell try," John replied.

"I need help," Dunchee said.

"Can't leave my uncle, Mr. Dunchee."

"Already talked it over with your uncle. It's all right with him."

John looked up sharply, "What you paying?"

"I'll treat you right," Dunchee said, stiffly.

John figured Dunchee meant he'd pay more money by the "right" business. The way John figured it later on, Dunchee must have bought him from his uncle because, when he went to work on the Dunchee place, Dunchee treated him just about like the slaves he'd bought over in New Orleans and brought into Texas to work for him before the Civil War. The other hands told John about this.

All the hired men were older than John, and they teased him a lot. He did not mind much because he kept thinking about the miserly twenty-five cents a day his ma was making in town, and figured he'd be able to help her out a lot more than he'd ever been able to do before.

It wasn't long before he was not only looking a pair of mules in the tail all day long, but he was milking seven head of cows both morning and night. As soon as he'd get through eating dinner he had to go out and chop firewood while the older hands rested a bit and smoked their pipes. He was forced out before daylight in order to get the cows milked in time for him to work in the fields. He got through so late at night he scarcely had time to get to bed before getting up again.

The other hands slept in a bunk-house—John slept in the barn. Even this, he didn't mind. He was so weary all the time he could have slept on a sharp pile of rocks.

John, in telling of it, apparently still felt the kicking around he'd gotten so long ago. "One of the hands kept calling me a second-hand nigger, figuring I didn't have any folks. I never told them a thing. One afternoon this

same man told me to fetch him a drink of water out of
the cistern. I never did like the sneer in the man's voice.
But then, too, it might have been the way the old man
had been ordering me around. Anyway, I told him to
go find the trail to hell—and stay on it. He jumped up
from beside the wagon-bed, where he and a couple of
his cronies were loafing, and knocked me flatter than a
skillet bottom. Then the dirty skunk kicked me in the
belly—saying he'd teach a boy how to act around his
elders.

"I was sure sore, in mind and body, for days. Later,
I laid for him by the bunk-house. When he came out
I hit him between the ears with a single-tree. He said
'ummph,' and fell over on his face.

"I ran like a rabbit and hid in some hay in the barn.
Old man Dunchee found me, and really reamed me
out. I was relieved to hear I hadn't killed the idiot
hired-hand—although I thought he deserved a good
killing. He left me alone after that deal.

"The end of the month rolled around, after what
seemed to be years. I was so anxious to be paid, I was
slobbering at the mouth. Then that ratty old Dunchee
handed me four dollars—saying that was all a boy like
me was worth. I walked out to the barn to brood.

"There in that damp old barn, I fingered a chopping
axe. I couldn't make up my mind whether I should go
in the house and cut old man Dunchee's head off, or

not. I was mad enough to do it, but somehow, I felt, there should be a better way."

"Just think," Long John grumbled to me, six decades later, "four dollars! Why the cheap old son-of-a-bitch! Four dollars for a month of working like a mule!"

He grunted, settled in his chair, and went on with his story. "I peeked through a crack in the heavy-timbered barn door. Maybe I *was* just a snotty-nosed kid, but I'd done a man's work, and I didn't aim to swallow that pill.

"The lamp-light went out, and I knew old tight-fist had gone to bed. About that time a thought struck me. Staked out in front of the house a ways, was a dandy bay saddle stallion. Well, I wasn't too sure about that, either. I'd heard of a feller being hanged over east for stealing a horse. *But Lord-amercy, four dollars!*

"The stallion threw his head up. I could make him out plain by ducking low. He snorted once, and I began to whisper to him easy-like. Pretty soon he calmed, and I rubbed his neck a little, and talked some more. He felt warm to my touch, and that gave me courage. I took the axe and chopped the stake-rope. Every time that axe struck, I quivered all over for fear Old Dunchee or some of his chicken-livered hired hands would wake up.

"I took the rope that was left over and made a half-hitch around the bay's nose. Then I jumped on him, belly first, and scrambled upright as the bay whirled

about. I wished then I'd managed me a saddle. But the
stallion hauled me off into the woods, fox-trotting to
beat hell. And I haven't been back to pay my respects
to Mr. Dunchee since."

II

"I RODE HARD for three days and three nights, taking very little rest," John talked on. "The bay was a sticker, and held up good under the conditions, but I knew we both had to rest. We camped—camped, hell—we had nothing to camp *with*. We slept in a bushy clearing, near a small stream.

"When I woke up it was dark. I was so famished I could have eaten a week-old cow-chip. I didn't know where in the world we were, except that we were many miles west of old Dunchee's. Knowing I would have a tough time foraging for food by night, I went back to sleep.

"It was daybreak when I awoke again. My belly was getting numb, and I had a sluggish feeling all over. The bay had watered and fed some, and wasn't quite so gaunt.

"Riding on west, we stumbled onto a big farm house. I knew by the large size and well-kept appearance of the barn that the man was a money-maker—a rare thing in that part of the country in those days.

"I rode around to the front of the house, and tied the bay to a tree. Suddenly the windows were full of heads—every one a girl's. I was scared witless, but so hungry I couldn't keep from knocking. I heard somebody yell, 'Ma, Ma, somebody's at the door.'

"Ma proved to be a fine looking woman—heavy, but scattered out better than my aunt."

The woman asked John in, and wanted to know right off what a young man like him was doing in this part of the country. Apparently she could tell, by the looks of the bay, that they had come a long way. Then, as was the custom, she asked if he had been to dinner. "I wanted to yell, Hell no!" John reminisced. "As loud as I could. But instead, I said, 'No Ma'am. I could do with a bite to eat.'

"She fried some sowbelly, and set out a big tin cup of milk and some cold biscuits. Good? The best I'd ever tasted. She ordered one of the girls to go out and take care of my horse. I was hoping they'd *all* go, but they kept circling around like hounds after a treed 'coon, talking in whispers, and giggling. If I hadn't been so damned hungry, I'd have choked on that very first biscuit.

"I figured the woman was going to question me, but she let it go when I told her I was riding west hunting work. She said her man, Charlie, would be back soon, and would probably have some work for me. Well, I was still too close to a country I knew I'd lost my welcome in, but I thought if I'd keep quiet and keep the bay out of strangers' sight, I might get by for a while.

"Charlie proved to be a good-natured sort of feller. I liked him right off. He wanted to know if I had had any experience breaking horses.

"I lied like sixty, 'Yep, lots of it.' "

"I'll give you five dollars a head for 'em, gentle-broke. You see, I need several for my daughters."

John was growing taller every day, but as he put it, "the skin lay awful close to my bones." At this time he probably weighed around one hundred and five. At first he had plenty of trouble trying to handle the wild broncs, but it wasn't long until he learned some things that made it a little easier. John explained his horse breaking methods this way. "I'd snub one up to a post in the center of the round corral. Then I'd take a rope and tie it around the horse's neck. From the same rope I'd make a loop around a hind leg and pull this up next to the horse's belly. When the ornery devil would buck and kick he'd trip and fall. The more he kicked, the more he choked. Then I would take off my shirt and shake it all over the bronc until he quit fighting. I kept this up until the bronc had learned not to kick or buck."

Julia, the oldest girl, stayed at the house while the rest of the family worked in the fields. She took to slipping out and watching John through the corral poles. They didn't say a word to each other the first few times. Then, John began to catch himself getting overly brave with the broncs—even to the point of showing off.

"I snubbed one up that had never been saddled and threw the leather on his back," John said, talking through his nose, and pulling at his long grey moustache. "He was humped up, and the saddle looked as if it had a cantaloupe under it. I untied him from the snubbing post, and crawled on at the same time. It was a three-year old blue roan. The crazy bronc didn't buck at first—kinda walked around stiff legged, as if afraid to move. Then the wild critter swallowed its head, and squealed. This was closely followed by some hard, fast, crooked bucking. I stayed on a while, then all of a sudden I looked down and there wasn't anything under me. I fell into the side of the corral, sliding to the ground like a bar of soap down a rub-board."

"Julia asked anxiously, 'Are you hurt?'

"No," I managed to answer.

"Then she climbed over the fence and helped me to my feet. I jerked loose, not wanting any help from a girl.

" 'Come on over to the house and have some sugar cookies and milk. I made the cookies myself,' she said.

"I went. Well, we talked a while about the horses

AFFIDAVIT

I, JOHN HARRIS DUNN, have told the story of my life to MAX A. EVANS for the purpose of writings. It is the truth from beginning to end. I hereby release any photographs of myself that he wishes to use in anyway connected with these writings.

J. H. Dunn

STATE OF NEW MEXICO)
)ss
COUNTY OF TAOS   )

On this 16th day of April, 1952, before me personally appeared J.H.DUNN to me known to be the person described in and who executed the foregoing instrument and acknowledged that he executed the same as his free act and deed.

IN WITNESS WHEREOF, I have hereunto set my hand and affixed my official seal the date and year in this certificate first above written.

M. Harper
Notary Public, Taos County, N. Mex.

Affidavit executed and signed by John Dunn before his death, testifying to the truthfulness of this book.

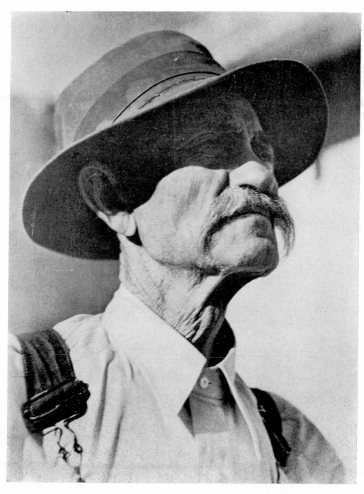

LONG JOHN DUNN OF TAOS

and this and that, and then Julia said, 'I wish you didn't sleep in the barn.'

" 'I don't mind. I'm used to that sort of thing.'

" 'Where is your home?' she asked.

"I lied to beat the devil. 'San Antone.' "

After that, the horse-breaking went easier. John liked her company, and she always gave him something to fill up the empty space in his belly.

He had four broncs working fine and was doing a little roping on two of them. Charlie seemed pleased, and paid John ten dollars.

"Just about the time I was getting to a point where I really liked it at Charlie's," John reminisced, "Julia started acting kinda funny. We went into the barn to drink some milk she had brought me, and she came over next to me and scooted up close. I slid away, and she slid with me. She was grinning—with a grin that seemed to me sorta silly-like.

"I drank my milk, and went out, saddled up a bronc, and rode around for a while, trying to figure out what in the hell was the matter with Julia.

"My bed was in the hay loft, and had two blankets, one under and one over," John confided. "One afternoon I was taking a little snooze on the sly. I opened one eye to check up, and saw Julia crawling over towards me. She was red in the face, and breathing hard. I threw the blanket back, and raised up. She jumped right up astraddle of me. I was scared plum to death—

and bucked like a locoed mare. She held on for a while, saying over and over, 'John! John!' I broke loose, and about half way down the ladder I fell off. I struck out on foot, and hid in the brush till supper. I was afraid Julia was going to kill me, and I figured it would be pure hell to be killed by a girl."

John said he wished he'd known then what he knew a few years later. He'd probably have worked quite a spell at Charlie's. As it was, he saddled up the bay, and rode away that night—still heading West.

III

AFTER WEEKS of riding across mesquite, chinery, sage and creeks of every size and color, John wound up at Pecos, Texas. He rested a couple of days, and learned there was plenty of work in the Big Bend Country south of Fort Stockton. There was.

John was already grown to well over six straight, lean, leather-tough feet, and the troubles he'd seen made his frosty blue eyes seem years older than they were.

He got a job on what was called the Half-Brothers' Ranch, owned by several Jews who kept residence in San Antonio. The ranch's southern boundary was the Rio Grande—a river which John was to contact again and again in the future—both downstream near the

Gulf of Mexico, and later hundreds of miles upstream in northern New Mexico.

Land scrips could be brought in Texas for as little as sixteen dollars a section (640 acres). All a rancher had to do was make a deal with a surveyor and he could pick his land. Of course, the primary wants were grass and water. The waterholes and river banks were, of course, taken first.

The Half-Brothers had bought thousands of acres of these scrips in anticipation of the future. Cattle were everywhere; all one had to do was to have a string of good horses and surveyed land and he was in the cattle business. These cattle were unbranded and, according to the law of the land, anything over a year old could be caught and put under the brand of the man handy enough with a rope to get the job done.

Until the first inkling of a market to the north, the cattle ranged mostly undisturbed. Indians, preferring buffalo to cattle, had left them alone. The cattle had migrated in from Mexico, where they had been imported centuries before. Both the cattle and the horses descended from European stock, without which this industry would have been vastly different.

They were allowed to go wild and "the survival of the fittest" produced cattle more noted for endurance and fleetness of foot than for tender cuts of meat. They were also adorned with an immense spread of horns which gave them a veritable pair of spears with which to protect themselves. Many a cowboy could attest to the wickedness of the projections. These wild cattle required even wilder men to handle them—a cogent reason for the development of the western cowboy into such a rough, tough breed of man. A three-year-old steer, weighing in the neighborhood of a thousand pounds, was fair game for the best of cowboys. He had speed to spare, and it seemed to be his special delight to race through the thickest brush. When and if a cowboy was fortunate enough to get his rope over the horns, he had a fight on his hands.

Cowboys usually worked in pairs. One would rope over the horns, and the other around the heels. John Dunn, in these years of the cattle drives, was to become a topnotch roper, and later was to win considerable money at rodeos. The Half-Brothers had hired every good hand they could get, and had put their brand on thousands of cattle. It proved to be an action of far-sightedness as the northern markets opened up.

In the fall of 1868, close to eighty thousand cattle had found market in Abilene, Kansas, and everyone was highly enthused over future prospects. Eastern states, especially the corn states such as Iowa, wanted cattle to feed and fatten on corn, for the eastern cities. The United States Army was anxious to fill Indian contracts with these Texas cattle. Private operators were in the market for "she-stuff" with which to start new ranches. Settlers from the prairies were ready to buy all the oxen they could get to break their lands for farming.

The town of Abilene quickly took on an air of frontier prosperity. As word drifted back of the excitement of trail drives, it became one of John's ambitions to make one. He was soon to get a chance.

Other points on the railroad quickly opened up. Dodge City, Kansas, rapidly replaced Abilene as a main shipping point. It became apparent the cattle business was entering a boom era. It wasn't long before eastern capital became interested. Even Europeans invested heavily in cattle. Companies were formed. Some ranches had holdings of an area over a hundred miles long and fifty miles wide. Ranches like the famous Matador and the XIT around Dalhart, Texas, in the northern panhandle, sprang from big business such as this.

The boom didn't really reach its peak until the 1880s. The frenzy swept across the northern and western half of the United States and extended into the British possessions in western Canada. Pasture lands the ranchers bought for a few cents an acre were readily sought at three and four dollars. Land soon became a premium, and most of the best of it was held by smart speculators. The Texas legislature had finally been brought into active operation. They enacted a law out of which grew the state's splendid system of education, giving alternate sections of land to the public schools, where thousands of oil wells are now pumping. John missed that part of his education, but he assuredly received plenty of the practical.

In time, barbed wire entered the picture, changing the West a great deal. Many bloody gun battles were fought over the right to fence a water-hole or a particular piece of land. The cattle were now confined to a certain area whether large or small, and the cowboys had a new job—ridin' fence.

The Half-Brothers paid twenty-five a month. John figured he had already ridden his way into heaven, drawing such big wages. He sent the first two months pay home to his mother. They put him to "riding line," which was riding the boundary lines of the ranch looking for tracks of stock that might have crossed over. The next job was going out and bringing them back.

John and another fellow were camped at a line-shack about thirty miles from headquarters. Headquarters would send out a wagon every six weeks or so with flour and such. They didn't need much grub because there was plenty of it all around them. When they were going to ride line for three or four days they'd take along a small bag of flour. Then they'd just ride up and shoot a cow, cut off whatever they needed for the meal, and tie some on the saddle for the next feed. Cattle were only worth a dollar in the area, anyhow.

"One morning five white men and two Yaqui Indians rode up to the line-shack," John remembered. "I saw right away they were Texas Rangers, and naturally figured they were after me. They weren't. The lawmen told us about a killing and robbery over north, and wondered if me or my partner had seen anything of the three men involved. I said neither of us had, but we would be glad to help. We saddled up and rode away with the search party.

"About four miles from camp, on a sandy ridge, one of the Yaquis found the trail. I remarked that the tracks looked as if they were only a couple of hours old. The Rangers thought so, too. But one of the Yaquis explained that they had been made in the dark of the night, and pointed out that the tracks went right through the center of the big clump of sagebrush. If it had been daytime they would have ridden around the bush because of the obvious openings on either side."

The Yaquis proved to be right, because a few days later the whole party returned. They had tracked to the Mexican border, but had never caught up with the outlaws. The Rangers stopped over for a while and had a meal with John and his cowpoke partner. They tried to make the Rangers feel welcome, but John didn't take a free breath until they were gone.

John and his companion wintered well, and in the early spring went into headquarters to get their pay. They had planned on making Fort Stockton for a little fun. John was made an offer, however, that stopped this immediately. A cow-buyer was going to trail a herd of two thousand steers through to Montana to the N-

Bar-N Ranch. He offered John thirty dollars a month and a bonus of fifty dollars if he finished the drive. John took him up.

The trail drive tested every good and bad quality a man had. During the trails of hundreds of miles across open spaces, the best or the worst was certain to come out. Day after day of eating the dust of the trail herd, rubbing saddle leather, watching for Indians or signs of anything that might cause a stampede, all went to make a man or break him. The long nights of staying on guard around the herd, when every bone and muscle begged for rest, then a few short hours of sleep on the hard, sometimes cold ground, with only a couple of blankets for a bed roll, was really a test.

"A feller learned to use a rope," John reminisced, "for more reasons than one." He spat, and wallowed his quid. "Sometimes it would save miles of hard riding after a steer, and it was always a good convincer when an ornery old steer wanted to make trouble. A rope, too, was handy to drag firewood to the cook, tie up a bronc—or even hang a man, if the occasion called for it." John's long fingers touched his skinny neck unconsciously as he told this. "Out of necessity, the man, the horse, the rope, the gun became inseparable."

John Dunn made a top-hand on the trail drives. He became an expert with both rope and gun. His long, lithe frame was as active as a cougar's and as tough as rawhide. By many hardships and narrow escapes, he developed a profound lack of fear. All of these were to combine in later years to great advantage.

The trail-drivers rode to Helena, Texas, where they trailed through to Henrietta, and from there over into Oklahoma (what was then Indian territory). To the Texans it looked like a Garden of Eden. Grass, two feet high, waved like wheat in the wind. There were all kinds of wild plums everywhere, dewberry thickets in bunches, wild pigeons and turkeys, deer and antelope by the thousands. Truly, it was a land of plenty.

The trail-drivers lived well off the wild game, and the cattle kept in fair shape from the plentiful grass, even though they had little time to graze. Two thousand head of steers cover a lot of country between the point and the drag. There were plenty of outlaws in the territory then, and they usually gave the trail-drivers more trouble than the Indians.

John was still a kid and kept a keener lookout for Indians than the older hands. One day his sharp eyes happened to catch a glimpse of something moving on a little ridge behind a clump of brush. He sensed, somehow, it wasn't a wild animal. He realized, too, that if he talked to anyone else he would give away the fact he'd seen something. So, after rounding the ridge, he took down a gully that circled in behind the suspicious object. He carried no pistol then, but he had a Sharp's buffalo gun.

John tied his horse in the gully, and slipped up to a brushy patch on the hill. What he saw wasn't an Indian, but a white man, armed with two pistols and a rifle tied to his saddle. He was getting on his horse, when John raised up and leveled the Sharp's at him. "Hold up there!" he yelled.

"The man stiffened; I started to shoot him," John recalled, "because it looked as if he were going for his pistol. The man changed his mind, and I slipped up behind him and told him to unbuckle his gun belt. He did. Then I took the rifle from the horse and walked him and the horse down to the gully. As we came into view some of the hands saw us. The boss and two more men came riding back to meet us hell bent for the election.

"From the trail-boss's questioning, we found out the man was scouting for a bunch of outlaws who were camped several miles east. The boss was surprised to hear that the badmen had planned to raid and take over the herd if the herd wasn't guarded by too many men.

"We talked it over, wondering if we should shoot him or not. The outlaw—said his name was Sam—promised to work for us into Caldwell, Kansas, free of charge, if we wouldn't shoot him. I told the boss I would keep Sam under close watch if he'd let him come along. The boss hesitated, but when two of the hands said they'd take a chance, the boss agreed. We took

Sam's guns away from him and hid them in one of the chuck wagons.

"Sam was a good-natured cuss, and he and I hit it off all right. Sam was wearing moccasins, and said he had run with a tribe of Indians before joining the gang of outlaws. His understanding and ability to get along with the Indians showed to good advantage one day when a bunch of about forty stopped us trail-drivers. He talked things over with the chief and said that for twenty steers or five horses the Indians wouldn't molest us. The trail-boss gladly gave up the steers because the horses were all-important and hard to keep."

Sam proved one of the quickest thinking fellows John ever knew in his life, and he used this incident to back up his belief: "One daybreak, after sleeping near the wagon, Sam crawled out of his bed-roll and while reaching under a blanket for his moccasins, a rattle-snake bit him on the left trigger finger. He ran over to the wagon, grabbed up the cook's hatchet, laid his finger on top of a wagon wheel, and without hesitating, chopped it off slick as a whistle. The cook gave him some flour which he held around his finger until the bleeding stopped. I killed the snake with a dead limb."

The men had several stampedes on the drive, but nothing serious in the way of cattle losses. One man was killed when his horse fell in front of a stampede. A coyote's howl or a lightning flash could make them run. After about the fourth time, the boss said he believed they'd have stampeded if they smelled an Indian a mile away.

When the herd reached Caldwell, Sam's guns were returned, and he was set free. By this time, the stub of his finger was practically healed. John asked him, "You need any money, Sam?"

Sam laughed, "I probably got more than all you fellers put together."

That was the last John ever saw or heard of Sam.

They trailed up to Dodge City without any events of importance. The steers were quarantined there for a month. It was claimed that they were diseased. John thought then that it was a racket to sell pasture at high rates. The town was wild, and the drivers had a hell of a big time there.

It was there John started watching the gamblers. And it was there he first acquired the gambling bug that was to stay with him to his death. Bat Masterson, marshal then, was having a rough time keeping the town under control. John heard several years later he had done a jam-up job of law enforcing.

While they were at Dodge City, a Texas cowboy, named John Dunn, who had never seen a train before, saw one and decided to rope it. His decision had been made after several hours in a Dodge City saloon. He roped it all right, right around the smokestack. It jerked him and his horse down, nearly killing them both.

—◦◦◄ 47 ►◦◦—

After watching the goings-on in Dodge City, John decided he'd buy himself a pistol as soon as he was paid. He did. But before John was paid they had covered lots of ground. Their delivery called for eighteen hundred head to the N-Bar-N Ranch on the Canadian border in Montana.

This was not the end of John's trail-herd days, however, for after returning to the Half-Brothers Ranch, he got a chance to go on another trail drive the following spring. The Half-Brothers outfit had made a deal to deliver twenty-eight hundred head of cattle to the Sioux Indians in South Dakota. John was happy to sign on, as the ranch life seemed rather dull to him now.

They left the ranch with two wagons, twenty-three cowboys (part of them Mexican *vaqueros*) and over a hundred head of horses in the *remuda*. Before the long drive was finished, they needed more horses and more men, as some of them quit on the way.

Twenty-eight hundred head of longhorn steers proved just too many steers to handle right. Before reaching Odessa, Texas (which was just a water stop then, but now a thriving oil town), they had been without water for the stock for three days. That country is covered with chinery brush, mesquite and what is not covered by this is sandy or hard eroded clay. It was hot even in the spring.

There was a set-up of extra long water troughs at Odessa, and the man in command there charged them a cent and a half a head to water. John found himself so busy working stock he never could remember where their water supply came from, or how. The steers' tongues were swollen, and they drank slowly. The cattle were all day watering.

Then they made their way across country, the country little different from that which they had just covered, on to Roswell and the Pecos River.

The herd was stopped at the Chisolm Ranch headquarters to hire more men, for several of the Mexican *vaqueros* had quit at Odessa. A day out of Roswell they bedded down at a small ranch house. The cowboys had a guest that night—William Bonney, or Billy the Kid, as you prefer. This later-to-be-famous outlaw was on the dodge at the time, but the Texans didn't know it. To John he seemed like a hell of a nice fellow. "He was as ugly as the devil, with his teeth sticking out in front like a mad beaver's," John later told a friend. "Nope, his face wasn't much to look at." John afterwards became acquainted with Pat Garrett, the man who finally killed William. The Kid reputedly killed his first man when he was twelve years old, for insulting his mother. Before he was finally shot in the back at the age of twenty-one years, he had killed a man for each year of his life.

The herd was pushed on across into Springer, New Mexico. It was hot country, with nothing in sight but rolling prairie and occasional mesa. Good water was to

be had there, but little else. The cattle were shipped to
Cheyenne by train, and driven from there to the Indian
agent at Standing Rock, South Dakota.

That was John's last go with the trail-herds.

He said, "I loafed around from place to place until
I was broke. I was tired of working for cow-outfits." He
gave as reason, "They didn't pay much then, and they
don't pay half enough now. How in hell they have gotten away with the starvation wages they pay their
hands is more than I can see. Maybe they *won't* much
longer."

John, now flat broke in Miles City, Montana, ran
onto a cowboy who had the same idea about cow-outfits
he did. Together they homesteaded a little place back
in the hills and, living off the country, constructed a log
cabin near a creek. There was plenty of wild game.
John told about stealing an axe in Miles City, "I figured
I'd have one hell of a time cutting logs with my bare
hands."

"Taking stock of the situation, me and my partner
decided our ranch made a poor showing without a cow
on the whole damned place. We made a plan that
would rapidly alter this set-up. Us would-be ranchers
built a corral back in a hidden canyon as far from anywhere as we could get. Then we built another corral
close to the ranch in the thickest brush and timber
around. After this we rode out and rounded up over
two hundred head of the best calves we could find.

John Dunn and one of his two-horse rigs.

Long John Dunn talking over old times with western horse-trainer
R. I. (Slim) Evans.

Plan was to keep the heifers, and sell the steers. We figured that, because the calves were unbranded, the poor little things were without owners. We overlooked the fact that the calves traveled alongside plainly branded cows. All this took some doing. A couple of sharper-eyed cowboys might have noticed these were the calves' mothers.

"We drove the *catch* into the previously prepared canyon. Calves, like babies of all kinds, have a strong tendency to bawl when separated from their mothers. This was the reason for our canyon hide-out. A bunch of calves bawling all at once will usually make a rancher ride like his tail was on fire to see what's the trouble.

"After some time our calves got used to being orphans, and me and my partner drove them to the homestead. As we penned them in the other corral I was sure we had a lot of gold on the hoof—but that's where I was wrong.

"At breakfast, three days later, we found ourselves surrounded by about twenty hopping-mad ranchers and their cowboys. It seems one man had accidently ridden upon our little herd of calves. From then on, things happened quick-like. These ranchers started to hang me and my cowpoke friend then and there. However, one of the gang prevailed on the others to take us to a small town where, as he argued, 'We'll have us a public hanging, because the judge will sentence 'em to hang anyway.' My skinny neck pained at the thought."

When they arrived there, the judge was out of town, and there wasn't any jail. So, the ranchers decided to hold the two overnight in a saloon. They soon tired of the waiting, and started drinking. By midnight they all were roaring drunk.

John recalled, "I nudged my partner (they hadn't even tied us up) and whispered to him, 'Let's make a break for it the next time they dance.' My pardner shook his head, 'No,' he said. I don't know why on earth, but he did.

"There was only one woman in the place. At first, they had taken turns dancing with her. Then the ranchers and cowboys started dancing with each other, and by themselves, to the music of the oldtime fiddle.

"It was plumb easy. I simply walked out. Before I crawled on my horse, I picked up a rope laying on the ground. It was only after I had ridden several miles into the wilderness I realized there was a strange horse tied to the other end of that rope!"

IV

John worked his way back into Texas, where his life took on many new and exciting aspects. The returning was a hard decision for him to make. He was almost certain they still wanted him for borrowing old man Dunchee's bay stallion, but he wanted to see his family, and was sorry he couldn't bring in some more money, being certain his family needed help.

John learned, upon his arrival, that Dunchee had been killed by one of his hired hands. He tried, unsuccessfully, to locate the man who killed him. "I wanted to buy him a new hat." John snorted, in telling about it. John's mother informed him that no charges were pending, since Dunchee had wanted his revenge to be personal.

However, all was not well. John's sister had married a drunkard, who beat her regularly. John had always been fond of his sister, and this new fact didn't sit well with him. He meant to investigate, however, before leaping into any new troubles.

But the whole deal was abruptly tossed in John's lap when his sister awakened him in the middle of the night, banging on the shack door. She was bleeding at the mouth. Her face was brutally cut from the blows she'd received. Hysterically she swore she would never return to the drunken maniac.

"I'm going over and blow the dirty bastard's head off," John told his sister. But his mother talked him out of it, insisting, pleadingly, that there was enough trouble as it was.

"A few days later I met the feller on the street," John bitterly told. "When I tried to question him, he hit me in the mouth. I went down in the street, but regained my feet before my brother-in-law had a chance to kick my head in. I'd already learned, the hard way, how to get up fast. He outweighed me by forty pounds, but I was a lot faster than he was. Also I was as mad as a mashed scorpion. I stepped in fast, and pasted him several hard punches. Before my brother-in-law could regain his balance I was out of his reach. My opponent was soon out of breath, and blowing like a foundered mare. I wound up, let him have my best punch square on the jaw, and he went back and down. His head struck the edge of a hitching rail. It made a funny noise—like dropping a wet sack.

"I went home. Told my ma and sister what had happened. Ma was worried, but my sister was almost dancing with joy. I hardly had time to relate the story before the law came and hauled me off. My brother-in-law had died. I was charged with murder. It was my first killing.

"There wasn't much I could do—no money, few friends, and although the dead man was a no-good sot, he had relatives in influential positions. I was sentenced to life imprisonment, and was escorted, with two more prisoners, to the state penitentiary that was then at Rusk, Texas. Three weeks I was there, before they could make up their minds what to do with me. All the time I was trying to figure out a way to escape. But, before I could form a plan, I was transferred to a prison farm on the Sabine River.

"I soon learned that files were being smuggled from the outside into the farm. Prisoners had long chains locked on their legs, which made a big raw sore before they could get used to dragging the chain. We couldn't pick these chains up, to walk, except by special permission from the guards.

"I got my file. Kept it hidden under my shirt. At night I worked away at the chain. It was a ticklish job, because if I filed too deep, the chain would come off and I would be exposed. If I cut too shallow I couldn't break the chain, if and when the right time came."

John still had no plan of escape, but knew he must rid himself of the heavy chain in any event. What was later to be called his "gambler's luck" soon presented him with an opportunity to escape. The skies clouded up and rained like a wrung-out sponge. The Sabine swelled to such flood depths that it threatened the whole countryside.

"All the prisoners were called out to work on a levee," John related. "I asked a guard if it was all right to pick up the chain. The answer was yes, and all prisoners were granted permission to do this.

"This was my moment. I strained against the chain, and it snapped. It was now or never. I raced down the river, hoping to reach the seclusion of the thick brush that abounded there. Two other prisoners, sensing that something was going to happen, had been watching me. They followed, but were slowed by their chains. I heard shots and screams. I figured the guards must have killed the other two.

"Shots were snapping all around me. I couldn't make much time in the sloppy, gooey mud. My only chance was the river. I dived in. While fighting to keep my head above water, my hands struck a big floating log, and I was borne down the river, clinging desperately to it. The guards couldn't possibly keep up in the mire. My luck had held."

It was some time before John was cast ashore at a bend in the river. He knew he was still in mortal danger, and that bloodhounds would be on his trail in a few minutes.

Staggering into the brush, he was about to fall from exhaustion when he spotted a farm house. This renewed his hopes, but if the residents were at home, he was in for more trouble. He took a chance and slipped inside.

"I had heard of an old trick from a fellow trail-driver," John grinned in the telling, "and I was willing to risk it, now. I gathered every can of pepper they had in the cupboard. (In those days people kept pepper and such supplies in large quantities.) Then I started out again. I scattered more than three cans of pepper on my back trail. I don't know what happened when the hounds stuck their noses to that—but I have a pretty good idea. At the time my only hope was that they would be turned into sneezing, mixed-up wrecks.

"Next few days were pure, unadulterated hell. I followed a railroad south. All the time I wanted to go west, but was afraid I'd get lost afoot in strange country. If it had been winter I would have frozen to death. I slept in the brush in the daytime, and traveled under the cover of darkness.

"Second day, I killed a rabbit with a rock, and ate part of it raw. Fifth day I raided another farm house. I was so hungry, and intent on getting food, the people were stepping on the front porch before I heard them. I crouched behind a big wood stove and nearly had heart failure when the woman came in and poked up the coals. It got plenty hot back there, and the sweat was about to drown me. She set something in a pot on the stove, and then they went out to do the chores. I stepped out, feeling like a baked apple. I took along a Sharp's rifle that was hanging on the wall, and ran out into the brush.

"I had lived in the brush and in hay-barns so much I didn't feel at home anywhere else. There was only one load for the rifle, and I didn't want to use it until I had to."

Two days went by without food and John still followed the general line of the railroad. He was forced to expend the bullet on another rabbit, but there was little left for him to eat except guts and hair, after the heavy Sharp's had hit.

The rifle was so heavy he started to throw it away, but a few minutes later was glad he hadn't. He heard a wagon and team coming down the wagon trail. Quickly he made up his mind to get himself a horse. When he stepped out in front of the wagon the driver yelled, "Whoa," and leaned back on the lines. "Want a ride?" he asked.

"Nope, I want to trade for one of those horses."

"Don't want to swap," the man said. "Helluva good team."

"Trade you this Sharp's," John bargained.

"Naw, I've got a gun," the man retorted, picking up one out of the wagon bed.

John said, "Let's see that gun."

"The damn fool handed it over barrel first," John recounted. "I reversed ends, and told him to crawl down out of the wagon. He jumped right off on top of me. I pulled the trigger and it clicked empty. Then I banged the man over the side of the head, and thought what a fool the feller was to ride around the country with an empty gun. Yet, if it had been loaded, I might have shot a hole in him as big as a silver dollar.

"I dragged him over to a fence, and took off his clothes. Then I exchanged my own dirty prison garb for the somewhat cleaner ones of the farmer. They didn't fit, but neither would the ones I left for him. I tied him up to a stump, with parts of the harness. He looked funny to me, sitting there in his long handles. Before I could unhook the horse, the farmer blinked his eyes and came to. He started yelling and raising old Billy.

"I said, 'Cool off, or I'll rap you over the head again.' I couldn't get it through the farmer's thick skull that he was just losing a horse, but if I didn't get out of this country in a hurry I'd lose my life. Besides, I left him a dandy, plumb empty, Sharp's rifle in payment.

"I figured I didn't make a very good picture of a cowboy as I rode away in the baggy clothes, mounted on a bare-backed work-horse that probably didn't know a cow from an Indian—but it was transportation."

John was to wind up in Matamoros, Mexico, where he would learn after hard and tedious study the art, or what to him was the business, of gambling. Later, he would use this knowledge as the basis for several fortunes all over the west.

V

OHN crossed the Rio Grande over into Matamoros, Mexico, broke and destitute. At that time the smuggling racket was going full blast back and forth across the Rio Grande. John found a man who knew the racket and threw in with him. They hauled their stuff to the United States by raft. This in itself was a treacherous business, the Rio Grande being full of dangerous whirlpools.

He and his partner were buying saddles, bridles, belts, shoes and other leather goods of all kinds, as well as fine silver and gold work in the form of jewelry, dinnerware and other decorative fashions. Shoes are an example of the handsome profit they made. The cost was fifty cents a pair in Mexico, and they resold them for over two dollars in the United States.

They smuggled everything they could lay their hands on with the exception of dope. John didn't renig from this because of any moral scruples. The weighty past he carried dictated caution. As it was, there proved plenty of competition for John and his partner, and many smugglers were apprehended.

Before too long, outlaws of every description were passing back and forth across the river. Among these was a fellow named Beech. He organized a gang, and was soon hard at work relieving the smugglers of their loot just as they would scramble ashore in the United States. This was a considerable short-cut for Beech, as he didn't have to worry about the purchasing of goods nor fording of the Rio Grande. Vultures were preying on the vultures. John and his partner escaped Beech's gang for some time by making their crossings in the middle of the night.

Beech finally caught up with them, however, and they lost a considerable amount of their profits. John later puzzled, "How he knew where and when we were crossing I'll never know. I had invested a fat lump of our bankroll in silver and gold work this particular trip.

"As we anchored our raft to a stump, by use of a heavy rope, several armed men encircled us. Beech did the talking, and to my surprise, he was a small, shaggy, almost meek-looking feller. I had heard so many tales about Beech, I naturally thought of him being big as a percheron horse.

"My partner made a move. It was the last one he ever knew about. He was shot plumb full of holes before he hit the ground. I don't think the poor feller actually meant to go for his gun. I think he simply meant to scratch his rump. Just the same, he fell dead right at my feet."

Beech acted almost sad about it, and apologized to John. John remained practically motionless while they loaded his gold and silver onto the backs of mules. As Beech departed, he laughingly said, "I'd like a load of good saddles the next time, if you'd be so kind." But Beech had put John out of business. There would be no next time.

John still had a little money Beech had left him, explaining that he didn't want to be responsible for John's starving to death. In spite of Beech, who was later killed by one of his own men, the smuggling racket continued. John steered the raft back into Mexico and something new.

Gambling was a big business in Matamoros, with so much easy, illegal money floating around. For the most part, gambling was honest in those days. The professional house or individual depended on the odds to win their money.

John played monte for three nights in a row and ran up a winning of several hundred dollars. He knew it was just plain kid-luck, but it prompted the owner to offer him a job dealing.

"You got good eyes and hands for the job," the owner said, "And you're big enough and mean enough looking to keep down trouble. How about it?"

"I don't really know anything about it," John told him.

"You'll learn," the man said—and John did.

"My teachers were masters," John proudly reminisced. "They took their degrees in greenbacks and gold. I specialized in monte. It was only a short time until I had a table of my own. I felt good about it because for the first time in my life I might get out of the brush and haystacks into a good bed and fine food.

"Our gambling was in a large saloon, and the bar was lined with smugglers, murderers, promoters, dope-peddlers, pimps and whores. The crowd was always raising hell, and a lot of fights took place. One I remember in particular, was between a whore and a smuggler. She was a good-looking woman and, outside of a coarse voice and vile language, could have fit into the most up-town society.

"She'd been going on with this man all day and into the night, loading him up with *tequila* while she herself was drinking a weak solution of cider. I watched the game between them, laughing to myself. The smuggler finally passed out, or so it seemed. She was reaching inside his vest, aiming to rob him, when he suddenly woke up and grabbed her arm. The man came up growling like a gut-shot panther, and threw her over his shoulder. She came down with a bang on the table. Two customers, not knowing and probably not caring what the cause of the fracas was, grabbed the smuggler from behind. While they held him helpless, the whore yanked a knife from a garter on her leg. She slashed furiously at the pinioned man's face. Before we could get to him, she'd cut his face until it looked like strips of jerky.

"The whore got a big hand, and the patrons went back to their drinking, feeling like it had been a good show. Personally, I thought she should have been hanged by the neck, and dumped into the Gulf of Mexico to feed the sharks.

"The customers gambled freely, knowing they could recuperate their losses across the border. Owner of the place was making a fortune. He later retired and built himself a fine home in Brownsville, where he lived until his death a short time back.

"One night a big Cajun from Louisiana was gambling at my table. He would stack three gold eagles then three Mexican silver dollars on top of them. When he lost he claimed only to have been playing the Mexican pesos. If he won he would shove out the whole stack. After one of these moves I refused to pay. The Cajun pulled out a knife from under his shirt and sliced me across the hand. See, I still carry the scar.

"The Cajun, realizing he had made a serious mistake, dashed for the door. Just as he was running through the swinging doors, I cut loose with one of those double-barreled shotguns. The Cajun's head was blown completely off. I could have whittled notch number two in my gun butt if I hadn't been afraid I might depreciate its value."

To John's notion, a shotgun was one of the best weapons made. At close quarters, ten to twenty feet, the charge of a wounded grizzly bear can be stopped. In the first place, a sawed-off double-barreled shotgun is short and can be swung into action rapidly like a pistol. Chances of a miss are small because of the spread of the shot. No time is wasted in taking aim. Loaded with heavy number one or zero shot, the shotgun is formidable indeed. A man struck with the full blast from this weapon is not likely to have the life left to fire back. This was always important, because many a man in the early days had been shot and killed after only wounding his adversary. With the double barrel, two lightning-like shots could be fired with one pull of the finger.

There were lots of rats in Matamoros. The four-legged and the two-legged variety. The shotgun took care of the two-legged species, but it took alley cats by the dozens to handle the others. The place where John worked kept seven or eight cats. It was necessary to continually replace them, as some of the patrons were cat haters and had no scruples about shooting them. John was no cat lover himself, and it didn't bother him to see a thinning out of these animals, although there were some who resented this treatment, and did all they could to feed and entertain the cats.

One gay night a group of men, mixing *tequila* with milk, had all the cats in the place stinking drunk. Not only this but they had extended the welcome to several homeless felines who were wandering about outside. The owner looked on all this with kindly tolerance, since most of the participants were good customers.

At first the cats stumbled about aimlessly meowing. One big old yellow tom-cat was a glutton, and drank until he looked as if he'd pop any minute. All of a sudden he raised his wobbling head and let out a squall such as only a drunken tom-cat can do. Then he raced across the room at break-neck speed, climbing up the wall until his head hit the ceiling. He would fall to the floor, and race across the room to another wall. Seeming to tire of this, he dashed down the length of the bar, still squalling, and overturning most of the drinks on his way.

"All the gambling and drinking had stopped," John fondly recalled, "and everyone was trying to catch that damned loco cat! Those who managed to lay hands on him were scratched to the bone. In the meantime, more cats had joined the chase, and those that didn't were all yowling. Noise and confusion became so god-awful that the bar was emptied, and business was bad the rest of the night. The employees finally managed to get all the cats outside, where they continued their party up and down the streets of Matamoros all night.

"Next night a sign hung over the bar—NO DRUNK CATS ALLOWED WITHOUT OWNER'S PERMISSION. Alcohol is bad enough on mankind, but what it will do to a cat is nothing less than terrible."

John had a room directly across the street. In it was a big soft bed, and every other night it had clean sheets on it. To him this was the height of good fortune.

"One night three women and one man entered the saloon," he recalled. "It was apparent that they had pull with my boss, because the word was passed to all hands to see that no harm should come to them from any of the trouble-makers or drunks. The youngest of the women made her way to my table and took up play.

"Now women, as a rule, are poor gamblers," John said, from over half a century of experience, "being interested as much in flattery and the thrill of the game as in winning. Once in a while a woman will make a good gambler by using her looks to advantage. One of these can really give a gambler fits. This one wasn't one of the latter. I won consistently, conscious of the fact that she was watching me more than the cards.

"I was very happy to see them leave. She smiled and said, 'I'll see you again, I hope.'

The man was the saloon owner's backer—a wealthy man from Brownsville. The young woman was his daughter. John soon learned that the man had made his fortune in contraband cotton during the Civil War.

Matamoros was the center. Since it is situated near the mouth of the Rio Grande, it was a natural for this trade. Texas cotton crossed the river anywhere for hundreds of miles above and was freighted down on the Mexican side to tidewater. The town did an immense business during the blockade of the seaports. Twenty dollar gold pieces were thicker than dimes are today. The cotton found a ready market at wartime prices, and safe shipment under foreign flags.

John's would-be girl friend, as it turned out, had a father who had had no compunctions about this type of business. He'd bought the cotton at interior points, then freighted it by ox-trains over the Mexican border, and from there down the river to Matamoros. Once he had the staple on neutral soil it was sold as a local product, and the Federal Government dared not interfere.

The man had made a fortune, but with all his money neither he nor his family were ever accepted into the high society of Brownsville. Their money got them nowhere in this line, even though they tried hard and long. They were all sorely disappointed. It wasn't so much that he had dealt in illegal goods that kept them out of select circles, but rather that he had been foolish enough to divulge and brag about his activities.

"About a week later," John went on, "the woman came back and strolled right over to my table. I was puzzled at first, but soon figured the woman had it sweet on me. We went out a few times, and although I enjoyed her company, I tried to avoid it as much as possible. Now, this may sound strange, but the woman was intent on getting hitched. I was not indifferent to the fair sex, but simply wanted to be single for the time being.

"The boss told me what a break I was getting, and thought I should latch on to her fast as possible. The hired hands kidded me quite a bit, and took to calling me 'Gentleman John.'

"She took up a lot of her time losing sizable amounts of her father's money. The more I tried to tell her there was no go between us, the more determined she seemed to be. Her father came over and begged her to leave with him, but it did no good.

"After a while she quit her gambling, and started drinking. Her eyes gradually sunk back into her head, and she lost a lot of weight. I thought it over carefully one night, and decided there was only one thing for me to do. Pull out.

"I bought a couple of good horses, and though I hated to take the chance, I rode across the Rio into Texas, leaving the woman in the bar getting quietly drunk."

VI

John rode through the country, stopping with Mexican people as much as possible. They treated him exceptionally well and, though he was sure some of them sensed he was on the dodge, none ever turned him in. Having a fair-sized bankroll, he managed to pay for their services.

His intentions were eventually to go to San Antonio and establish himself in the gambling business there, but for the time being it would be wiser to avoid the big towns. He still remembered the leg-irons at the State pen.

But by the time he reached West Texas, the homesteads were few and far between. John's bankroll had grown smaller every time he put a hand in his pocket. Finally he went broke, but somehow, in the process, he had managed to acquire a string of five horses. Having been on the trail pretty steadily, he was anxious to let the horses have a rest and good feed; and he needed a little care himself.

As John put it: "I rode up to a little rundown shack and yelled. A man stepped outside and asked me to light and hitch. I got right to the point, and told him I'd like to work a few days so my horses could rest. The man was a bachelor, and took me up on my offer right off, admitting he was a bit behind with the work. He sure wasn't lying. Everything that could be seen needed fixing. The weeds had just about taken over the place.

"He put me to doing the odd chores. He was a hog-raising man, and I had to spend a lot of my time patching the hog pens and carrying water to them from a spring about two hundred yards from the shack. After a day or two he really got rough on me, and treated me more like a servant than a fellow who was in a tight spot for rest and grass. The horses were picking up some, but I wasn't gaining an ounce.

"One day after he'd been pretty rough on me, I decided to have a little fun with him. I was coming from the hog pen, picking at the tall weeds along the path, when the idea hit me. I tied several of the green weeds together across the path in different places. Then I went back and kicked one end of the hog pen down and started yelling as loud as I could, 'The hogs are out, Andrew! The hogs are out!'

"Andrew came charging down the trail like a cavalry colonel. He hit the first tie and slid forward on his belly like a snake. Then he got up and tore out again. I kept yelling louder and louder, and he was running and falling harder every time. When he finally reached the hog pen I had the hogs back in, and was fixing the pen.

"Without looking up, I asked him what took him so long. I told him I really had hell with the old red sow. I still didn't ever look up.

"Andrew was so out of wind he couldn't answer. He snorted, turned, and started slow-like back down the hill, shaking his head. I don't believe he ever realized what happened."

Andrew's skinned spots were several days healing. His temper wasn't healed any, either. John claimed he really got mean after that, but there wasn't much he could do but take it—until the horses were in shape.

Because the horses were picking up, the homesteader knew John wouldn't be there much longer, so he decided to clean out an old well near the house while he had help, thereby saving himself a lot of water hauling. They set up the windlass. He went down in the well, and John stayed on top to draw up the buckets as he filled them.

They worked along fine the first few buckets, then Andrew got to cussing and complaining because John had dripped a little mud on his head. Old Andrew was the kind of fellow who just couldn't be pleased, so John studiously ignored him, listened to far off things and let his mind roam at will.

About that time the homesteader decided he needed a rest, and ordered John to pull up the ladder so he wouldn't be so cramped. Obediently John did so, and Andrew was quiet for a minute or so. Then he roared up for John to go water the old blind horse. It had just dawned on him that John was getting a little rest, too.

"I could hear the old horse behind the house," John said, laughing through his nose as he told it. "He had a bell around his neck. Instead of going after water, I decided to go get the bell. With the bell hanging loosely in one hand, I walked slowly towards the well. Andrew heard it coming, and began to yell, 'John, run that old blind horse away from here. John, do you hear me? I said, run him off, before he falls in here on me. John! John, damn your worthless hide, drop that water-bucket and get that bell-tinkling old son-of-a-bitch away from here! John. Shoo, horse! Shoo, you old devil! Haaarrr, get outa here! Oh Lord, please don't let him fall in here on me, Lord! Poor old horse, Lord! He ain't never done nothing, Lord. He don't deserve to die this way, Lord! Lord, I ain't been so bad either that I deserve to go this way!'

"Then he really got worried and broke down," John trumpeted. "You never heard such goings-on. Andrew started throwing hands full of rocks out of the well, and crying a little, and praying a lot. I decided to give him a rest, so I slowly walked away. Andrew got awfully quiet, so he'd be sure the horse was leaving. Then I started back, but changed my mind. I figured the old bastard had had enough. I was almost sick from holding my laughter, anyway. I let Andrew have a good rest, and then buckled the bell back on the horse. Then I went back to the well.

"Andrew rasped out, 'Where in the hell have *you* been?'

"I replied, 'The old red sow got out again. Why, is something wrong?'

"Andrew just cursed a little under his breath and started digging.

"After the well was cleaned out, I left him, and headed north."

VII

I<small>T WAS</small> three weeks before John found himself in Mobeetie, Texas, in the northern Panhandle. He'd had plenty of time to think things over, and realized he was getting exactly nowhere. He also reasoned he wouldn't stand much of a chance in business because of an almost total lack of formal education. But he knew he could do all right gambling—if he could get out of Texas, and away from the law.

Transportation! That's what John wanted to do in a way of a business for himself. The need for it had been over-emphasized in his case. He could just see himself in the transport business, all set up with fine horses and good coaches. These things were on his mind when he rode into Mobeetie.

"It happened," John remembered, "that a three-day rodeo was in progress. I didn't have any money to enter any of the events, but I sure had the urge. I sold all my horses except one, and joined the fun. I was young, wiry, and eager, and had no trouble entering myself as a rodeo contestant.

"Calf-roping in those days was different, in that the roper stood his horse on a line, out in front of the calf, instead of in a chute behind it.

"I was all set in the saddle, ready for my first roping. Over-anxious, I missed my first loop. I spurred up beside the calf, bent over, grabbed its tail and turned it a flop. I jumped off and tied in fast time. The judges, however, disqualified me—saying I had to rope, not tail, the calf.

"I was disappointed, but went on into the bronc-riding about half-mad. I drew a big black gelding called *Ace-in-the-hole*. The bronc came out running, and never bucked a jump, although I was kicking out the top of his mane.

"Things were looking pretty low as I got astride a big red steer. It was my last entrance fee, and I *had* to win. Unlike *Ace-in-the-hole* the steer really turned on, and I took second money.

"Next day my luck changed, and I took first money in calf-roping, and drew second in steer and bronc-riding. It had been a long time since coins had jingled in my pockets. I had myself a big time in town that night.

By now I was feeling much better. I started a blackjack game, and picked up forty more dollars.

"Last day of the show, just before my turn came to rope, a couple of deputies walked up and put the arm on me. It seemed that one of the horses I had sold recognized its former owner, who happened to be passing through the country.

"I could already feel that leg-chain dragging on my skinny ankle. I wasn't recognized as an escapee right off, but I knew that would come directly. I was hauled off to jail.

"Next day, while the judge was thumbing through his book in preparation to sentence me, it came to me that I didn't like the surroundings. I took two long leaps and jumped through the window. I nearly broke my neck as I fell outside, but luckily didn't get a very bad cut from the broken glass. Somebody fired a miss at me as I ran into the crowd.

"I hopped myself a good, fast-looking horse—not taking the time to look around and ask its owner if I could borrow it. Riders, guns blazing, came boiling out of town after me, but I had a good start, and held it. I'll always remember that horse, because he was a real sticker. If he had ever faltered I would never had the pleasure of relieving so many people of their gambling money in the years to come.

"I rode right on into the night—hungrier and thirstier than a panic-time hobo. Early next morning I rode into

a wagon camp ground. Only one man was in sight. I
had already been seen, so I rode right up.

"The man said, 'Get down and have some grub,
stranger.'

"I said, 'Glad to.'

After eating, John told his plight. The man was in
complete sympathy. He suggested John turn his horse
loose and hide under some hay in his wagon. He had
been talking about a gold mining boom at Elizabethtown in northern New Mexico. John decided that Elizabethtown would be just the place for him, too. So he
turned his horse loose, and followed the man's sugges-
tions. The man's name was Tom Holder. His son is a
noted state game warden in the Taos, New Mexico area
now.

All day John would ride, nearly smothered under the
hay. At night he'd crawl out for a little air and grub.

Two days later they were stopped by a group of
Texas Rangers. They were hunting John. They asked
all sorts of questions, but Tom Holder did some smooth
talking. John was sure they could hear his heart pound
at his ribs.

Sometime after this they pulled into Elizabethtown,
or E-Town as it was commonly called. John gave his
humble thanks to Tom Holder then, and continued to
do so until the day he died.

Holder went to work in a placer mine, and John went
out to look for a spot to gamble. John soon discovered

LONG JOHN DUNN OF TAOS

that the town marshal here was also on the outs with the law in Texas. John propositioned him to go in partnership with him in the saloon and gambling business. The marshal gave John three hundred dollars and told him, "Win enough to set us up in *real* business."

Many years later John told about it: "I did just that. I sat in a big poker game that night. I really played my best. I had cards in my sleeves, my hat, coat and anywhere else I could stash 'em. So did everybody else that knew how. When the game broke up next morning, me and my partner bought the very saloon the poker game was held in."

The gold boom had first started in E-Town in 1866, when a drunken prospector camped next to a sloping rock. He had built a fire next to the rock to fry up some wild game. Suddenly he noticed gold oozing out of the rock from the heat of the pitch wood fire. He worked several days; digging out around nine thousand dollars in gold; but his thirst for alcohol soon drove him down to Taos. There, after consuming several long gulps of *vino*, he blurted out the whole story. Word spread all over the country, and the Elizabethtown boom was on.

The Indians had known about this gold for a long time, and decades before had spread the word to Bent's Fort, but it remained for the drunken old prospector to really set the thing going.

It wasn't until 1869, however, that a truly big discovery was made. A fellow named Hamilton stumbled onto a bonanza at a bend in a small gully. It was just out of town, and had been overlooked for years by the other miners. In all, over five million dollars in gold was removed from this one mine alone. It was common in those days for people to pay their bills in gold.

In 1887 Congress confirmed a huge land grant in favor of one Lucien B. Maxwell. This included most of the mining country around E-town. The company, with the backing of the U. S. Government, demanded twenty per cent of all minerals in the area. This cut so deeply into the profits of the mine that it started what was known as the Grant War. Miners rebelled, and went armed and ready to blow holes in any of the Grant employees. It created a bloody mess in the nine thousand six hundred feet elevation of E-town.

A young Eastern doctor, Dr. Martin, who later was to become a close friend of Long John in Taos, arrived on the scene. He was the only doctor in the country, and his business really boomed. He patched more bullet holes in those days than doctors give pills now. The lives he saved are unnumbered. All the old-timers speak today with respect and great admiration for Doc Martin.

The mines kept on operating for a number of years through sheer force and gunsmoke. E-town wasn't actually named until 1894. A miner by the name of John Moore had a beautiful daughter named Elizabeth. Everyone was familiar with and more or less awed by

TAOS OLDTIMERS

Left to right: Mr. Crandell, an Indian agent; old Don Juan Santistevan, the first banker and wealthiest man in Taos County; far right, Eloys Schuerich. House in background is Kit Carson's old home. The Carson home is still standing.

Long John Dunn watching modern transportation roll up what was once
his old stage coach trail.

her beauty, so it was only natural that they call the town Elizabeth.

Business was good, and John had complete protection, since his partner was the marshal. Lots of money floated around, not only because of the mining boom, but also because a large number of outlaws, thieves and robbers were hiding out in the vicinity. Some of those boys made solid wages with their six-shooters, and they all gambled freely.

One day three men, armed with revolvers and saddle guns, rode up. Before tying their horses they looked up and down the street, then entered John's saloon. They wanted to play monte, and since John specialized in the game, he tried to oblige them.

Long years later, John recreated the men in his sharp old mind—talking through his nose, and living again those wild days he'd been so much a part of: "I won over three thousand dollars from those toughies, without half trying. One of 'em was almost as tall as I was, and he had a black beard, and long black hair that stuck out from under a wide-brimmed black hat. He had black eyes, too, that were as mean looking as a bobcat with two feet in a number-four steel trap. My game-mates rested awhile and downed a few drinks, and then one of 'em went outside and brought back two buckskin bags full of silver. I licked my chops at that load of boodle. I always liked to set a lot of silver on the table in front of me all the time. That's the main reason my table always got the biggest play. It was like flies after molasses syrup. But then I saw that some of this money was blackened and bent. It meant one thing to me. It had been blasted out of somebody's strong box, and I was ready to bet my front seat in hell that box hadn't belonged to the three gents.

"Well, I never tried so hard to lose in my life. These boys had me hemmed in—three to one. They had two pistols apiece, and I figured they knew how to use 'em. I was ten feet from my shotgun, and I knew I didn't have any more chance getting to it than a one-legged man would have in an ass-kicking contest.

"They weren't any too happy about losing all their loot, and began to get a little restless. I thought fast, saying, 'You fellers just go over there and pick up whatever amount of money you need.' They all looked at me, and I damn near stopped breathing. Then the black-eyed feller said, 'Well, we could use a hundred apiece.'

" 'Hell, just take it!' Here was the first time in my life when the money was going the other way, and I was tickled flat about it. From then on, for the rest of my life, I made an oath to have that sawed-off shotgun of mine where I could reach it without untracking."

After they were gone John made inquiries as to their identities. He was informed that it was Black Jack Ketcham, the famous train robber, and a couple of his men. He remembers them calling one of the group Franks.

Several days later a horse backer came by and left John three hundred dollars. Black Jack had paid his debt. Jack paid his debt to society a few years later while robbing a train, single-handed, in Union County, New Mexico.

Black Jack and his gang robbed and killed all over Arizona and New Mexico for years. They were a hard, desperate, hunted band. At Folsom, New Mexico, the Colorado & Southern train had to slow to a stop on a long curve. It was easy for Black Jack and his gang to step aboard. On September 3, 1897, they did just that, pistols drawn.

Black Jack knocked out the Express messenger with the butt of his pistol. After warning off conductor Frank Harrington, they got away with several sacks containing over thirty-five hundred dollars in gold and silver coins. Posses were rounded up and sent out to scour the hills, but the outlaws made good their escape.

A short time later this same gang pulled the same robbery at the same place. Conductor Harrington was ribbed unmercifully about his 'pals' the train robbers. Harrington bought himself a shotgun, and swore it would never happen again.

On August 16, 1899, at one o'clock in the dead of night, Black Jack stepped back on the train alone, and armed with a rifle. He held the engineer and fireman at bay. He shot Fred Bartlett, the mail clerk, through the mouth, blasting out some of his teeth and scarring his face for life.

Harrington ran through the cars, knowing something was wrong, because of the unscheduled stop. Then he saw two men working at the coupling to unhook the the cars. Black Jack whirled and fired. At the same instant Harrington cut loose with the shotgun. Black Jack missed, and staggered through the door, and out into the night—his arm full of buckshot.

Next morning a posse and several officers found Black Jack sitting on the rail bed, his right arm tied up in a black silk handkerchef, blood-soaked, weak and pale. At the Nun's Hospital in Trinidad, Colorado, forty some odd buckshot were removed from his arm. After nine suffering weeks he was taken to the prison hospital in Santa Fe. Dr. DesMarias, the prison doctor, amputated the arm without the use of anesthetic simply because Black Jack refused it. Jack came through with enough spirit to tell the doctor, "I hope I can do the same for you some day."

Black Jack went on trial at Clayton, in Union County, New Mexico. He was finally sentenced to hang at Clayton Courthouse on April 26, 1901. The hangman built a special scaffold for Black Jack's long, heavy frame. He made the platform with a drop of eight and a half feet instead of the usual seven. A huge crowd gathered from miles around to see the death of Black Jack.

Jack howled to the hangmen, "Whip up, boys, I'd like to eat dinner in hell." He refused the ministrations of the church, and when the black hood was pulled over his head and the rope was tightened, the hangman asked if he was ready. Jack said, "Let 'er go!"

She went all right, and when the heavy body dropped, a great gasp came from the wild-eyed crowd. The long drop had jerked Black Jack's head off his shoulders, and the bloody object rolled out on the platform. A grin still seemed to be on its face.

The photos of this hanging, or head-jerking, can be seen today in the Eklund Hotel lobby in Clayton, New Mexico.

Long John's comments about it were ironic. "That could have happened to me if I'd been caught so long ago down there in Texas and other parts of the West. I kinda hated to hear about Old Black Jack getting it. He was such a damn good loser at monte."

When winter came to E-Town, they couldn't get anyone to carry the mail to Taos. John volunteered. Moreno Valley, and its snow drifts, have always been something to see, but bucking those drifts was something else. Somehow John made it through every time.

John was doing well in E-Town, but the several U. S. marshals sent there to control the war between the miners and the grant, put fear in his bones as to eventual discovery.

VIII

In 1889, John rode through what is now Eagle Nest Lake—but was then called Therma—and up through Taos Canyon, and into Taos Valley.

In Taos John checked up, and found that the ancient community was without any means of public transportation, except a branch line railroad which ended about thirty miles west of town. Somehow he knew this was it. The town was seventy-five miles from Santa Fe and eighty miles from the Colorado line. Here was plenty of room for an enterprising livery business. First, he had to have the money. John was making a good living in E-Town, but somehow he couldn't seem to get much ahead, and the fear of the law had kept eating at him.

He rode into the town he was to dedicate his life to, sitting straight as a lightning-rod in the saddle—a man six foot and over, with long, powerful arms, and gambler-quick hands. He also wore the busted nose he had suffered when he ran under a tree in the dark, up in Montana. This long, crooked proboscis was already his trade mark—through it he laughed and talked with a nasal-twanged voice that was to be imitated by hundreds later when telling some yarn about Long John Dunn. He wore a wide brimmed white hat, high-top boots, and he had just started what was to become a magnificent and well-kept mustache.

John was physically clean, and whenever possible, he bathed and shaved every day. In a way he probably was making up for all the times he had slept on the cold, hard ground with one long pointed ear awake for the sound of oncoming hoofs. He cared little for fancy dress, but he did like well-made clothes, and he wanted them clean. In later years he wore Pendleton western-wear, made out in Pendleton, Oregon, mainly because they were the best, and because his good friend and merchant Gerson Gusdorf handled them in his store.

When he dismounted and surveyed Taos plaza he saw a town lifted up out of mud. Ninety percent of its construction was of adobe, and was mud plastered. Burros, with loads of wood, and teams of wagon horses, stood tied to the hitching posts encircling the inside of the plaza. Numerous Indians, blanketed and silent, stood watching. But mostly there were the Spanish-Americans, who were soon to learn, if not fear, or at least lastingly respect, the one they were to name *Juan Largo de Taos*.

John didn't know then, when he looked around Taos plaza, that he was looking upon a town which was later to be known the world over for its artists and other cultural interests. Nor did he ever dream what a key part his transportation business would play in its development.

So John moved to Taos. He was followed by a bartender, and another gambler, from E-Town. They were soon in business; the gaming business.

The Taos before John's time was one of unexcelled excitement and adventure. It was almost inconceivable that such a man as John could come to Taos and later be responsible for that other phase of growth and development which would reach across the American continent and into European art circles. Taos had been bathed in blood over and over in the early days.

The pueblo of Indians, anciently established, but near the town, and a group of natives, rebelled against the American occupation. One such battle ended with ox-carts piled high with Indian and Spanish dead.

In June, of the year 1846, an American army was dispatched out west with a group of 1600 men—the Army of the West. By the time the force had reached the

New Mexico border, word had come to the ears of Don Manuel Armijo, governor of the territory of New Mexico. He prepared to defend Santa Fe.

The army took the city of Las Vegas without opposition and pushed on into Santa Fe plaza, with little or no difficulty considering the potential of the native forces. On August 22, 1846, General Kearny raised the American flag above the adobe-surrounded plaza of old Santa Fe—thereby declaring New Mexico officially a part of the United States. But soon word of resentment, in the form of dangerous uprisings, came to him from Taos about seventy-five miles to the north. Charles Bent, who had been a merchant and trader in Taos for many years prior, was appointed governor of the area, and was sent to investigate.

Shortly after arriving at his home in Taos, a large group of furious natives and Indians gathered in front of his home. Governor Bent had been warned of danger, but due to the past respect he had enjoyed in Taos, he couldn't bring himself to believe his friends would actually turn against him. The crowd grew, and soon filled the area across the street, where John Dunn was later to build his fine home.

The cursing and noise grew. Mrs. Kit Carson, and Mrs. Boggs, were trapped in the home with Governor Bent's family. His ten-year-old son, showing great courage, took a shotgun from the wall, and said, "Father, let's fight them." Governor Bent disarmed the boy, and went out in the patio to try and pacify the crowd. In the meantime, Mrs. Carson, Mrs. Bent, Mrs. Boggs and the children dug through the wall with a poker, to the house adjoining theirs. But this house was also surrounded.

Cries of the crowd became louder. Governor Bent staggered back inside, bolted the door, and crawled into the room with the others. They looked in horror at his freshly scalped head and his still breathing body. He collapsed in a pool of blood, and soon died. The rest were trapped in the house all night with his dead body. The family was there for over forty hours before friends broke in, and led them to safety.

During the time they were trapped, the rebels had attacked Turley's Mill, twelve miles from Taos, and killed seven men. To the southeast, at Mora, another band trapped a group of traders and slaughtered all eight of them.

General Kearny swiftly sent Colonel Price to Taos with a regiment of American soldiers. The main body of rebels holed up in a thick-walled church at the Pueblo. Colonel Price surrounded the entire pueblo to prevent escape. A large body of troops took cover about three hundred yards from the north wall of the church. Lieutenant Dyer, in charge of an artillery battery, moved up a six pounder and two howitzers. At nine o'clock in the morning all guns opened up, catching the church in heavy cross fire. The thick adobe walls held to a great degree, and Colonel Price, becoming impatient, ordered Captain Burgwin and a company of men to attack. The battle slots in the church spit out lead in a deadly volume, along with scores of arrows and spears that found flesh to penetrate.

Captain Burgwin, battling valiantly, was killed, and the whole company practically annihilated.

Finally by three o'clock that afternoon the Americans managed to get a six pounder within fifty yards of the western wall of the church. After ten direct hits in close proximity, the smoke-filled, blood-splattered church was opened up enough for the soldiers to take it. Some rebels escaped and joined other groups trying to escape out the northwest part of the pueblo into the nearby mountains. Captains Slack and St. Vrain pursued with their men, and ran down fifty-one rebels, whom they shot and killed, leaving only two who escaped.

That was the end of the battle except for the rebel leaders (between fourteen and twenty of them), who were shot before a firing squad. The soldiers had lost Captain Burgwin and seven other dead, as well as forty-five wounded. But the back of the rebellion was broken.

But it was the mountain men themselves, not the soldiers, led by such a personage as Kit Carson, who left the most romantic memories of Taos. They came from Texas, from Arkansas, from all over the west to hunt and trap the beaver and other valuable fur-bearing animals. They were a tough breed of men—more from necessity than by birth. The long months in the cold, mile high mountains, sleeping on the ground, riding or walking miles each day over the long trap lines, toughened them physically. And the ever-present danger, many times actual battles with the Indians of the area, toughened them mentally.

Kit Carson built up such a reputation as a hunter and fighter that it is hard to distinguish fact from fiction, but it is known that although he was a deadly shot with a rifle and downed more than his share of redskins, he had a genuine fondness for them and only shot when attacked or in grave danger. He learned to speak their language, and on many occasions took up for them. They developed great respect for him, and probably for that reason he survived to die a natural death as an old man.

In the off-season, the trappers would descend on Taos, where dark-eyed, free-wheeling *senoritas* awaited their pleasures. The older Spanish condoned this because it was simply a matter of business. The mountain men made big money and tossed it away in a big manner. The Taos business men furnished them with gallons of liquor at their own prices, of course, and before the mountain men had exhausted their stay the business people would have most of their money.

Many huge celebrations, called *fandangos*, took place when they were down from the mountains. It was a mad mixture of the colorfully dressed *senoritas*, the wild, strong, impatient mountain men, Spanish music and *vino* by the barrel. The men danced, drank and made merry with the women until they fell from exhaustion or wine. Sometimes these *fandangos* would end in a glorious battle between the younger Spanish men and the mountain men. The trappers seemed to enjoy this almost as much as the wine and women. They would sail in, swinging clubs, rifles, fists or anything else. Blood would fly, and the Spanish cut many mountain men to the bone with their sharp knives. It was all part of that keyed-up time in history which the mountain men did more than their share to preserve.

Kit Carson, like John Dunn, made Taos his home. The dwelling still stands today as a museum. He married a beautiful Spanish girl who was the sister of Governor Bent's wife.

It is plain to see that John had moved into a place that had offered much in the past, and he was going to see that it had much to offer in the future. But before he could bring this about he had to suffer some, wander thousands of miles across the wild west, and miss death by inches many times.

At Taos Junction, at the end of the branch-line railroad, a man named Meyers had built a bridge across the Rio Grande River, connecting Taos with the railroad. John could see the possibilities of his transportation dream coming true here. He made up his mind right then and there about his dream. Here in Taos was where he would make that dream come true. As he later said, and was quoted in the local newspaper, "I could just see myself sitting up there, with a big fine office, and my skinny stilts propped right up on top of the desk with a big black stogie shoved between my teeth. I would have stables full of good stagecoach horses, hotels and gambling houses all over the area. It would be Long John Dunn himself that would be haulin' everybody, everywhere, and it would be Old Long John himself rakin' in the silver."

John tried to buy the bridge. Meyers wanted fifteen thousand dollars for it. John had only four thousand. That was a long way from the needed sum. Business had not been extra good, and it had taken most of John's money to get started in Taos.

John went back to gambling in earnest, dead set on owning the bridge that would someday transport notables from all over the world to the historic old town of Taos.

It was still territorial days when John first arrived in Taos, and one had to have gambling licenses then. John managed two licenses—one for the game where the Don Fernando Hotel once stood, and the other for the game in a saloon where the Safeway Store now stands. John's partner, A. I. Polk, and John, ran both places.

There were about twelve *gringos* in Taos at this time. The rest were Spanish-Americans, Mexicans and

Indians. The town marshal was a Mexican who hated
all *gringos*. Juan Largo, as the Mexicans named him,
became one of the marshal's pet peeves.

John recollected one serious run-in with this branch
of the law: "One night, after consuming a quart or so of
Taos Lightnin', the marshal decided to rid the town of
all *gringos*. He stumbled up to my table, and with the
barrel of his pistol, raked a pile of coins off onto the
floor. As he turned to leave, he said he was going to run
every *gringo* out of New Mexico. I told my partner that
I figured he was taking in too damned much territory.
The other boys agreed with this."

The drunken marshal soon returned, through the
front door, and shooting. Some of his deputies had
come in the back way, and grabbed the young bartender's arms. John always refused to give the bartender's
name, as the man later held an office of high importance
in the public services. In fact, he was later to head the
police department in one of California's largest cities,
and retire after twenty-two years of service.

John yelled for the young man to hold still. He knew
if the bartender struggled the drunken marshal would
most certainly kill him. Gunfire blazed in the room.
When all was quiet, the marshal was lying with three
bullet holes, from three different guns, in his body, and
half his neck was gone from a shotgun blast. John always kept a sawed-off shotgun around in those days.

Old-time crew start construction on Servietta railroad station, where John Dunn met the trains, and hauled the passengers to Taos in his horse-drawn stage-coach.

John Dunn, in the last years of his life, looks with affection upon the bridge he built and made famous.

Dr. Martin, who had moved to Taos from E-Town, came over and cut the bullets out. John said, "Doc, I don't know why you're going to this trouble, because I'm sure the marshal don't give a damn now."

For some odd reason the natives decided that the young bartender was to blame for the killing, and took up the cry for his blood. It was almost a second revolution. John recalled, "I told the boys I didn't feel as if we could whip a hundred to a hundred and fifty mad natives, so I slipped him out the back, and hid him that night in an abandoned well.

"Next morning, before sun-up, I hauled an old trunk out of town in my wagon bed. Crowded into that trunk was the young bartender."

THE MINES were forced to close at E-Town because of the twenty per cent cut asked by the Maxwell Land Company. Then a discovery was made at Red River, a few miles to the west. John immediately went up there and put in a saloon. He still had his business in Taos to look after, so he hired a man by the name of Jess Wilson to run his new Red River establishment.

"Now, I ain't no drinkin' man, John," Jess said.

"Well, I don't give a damn whether you drink or not," John replied, "but no drinkin' man is goin' to work for me."

Profits were good at first, but they quickly slowed down. John headed for Red River one night, and walked into his saloon with both hammers back on a two-row, sawed-off shotgun. The place was full of miners, outlaws, and scalawags in general. It was obvious to John what was happening to his profits. Wilson was so drunk he could scarcely stand up to the bar to serve the drinks. The patrons weren't paying for half what they got.

John eased the hammers down and cracked Wilson over the head. Wilson fell with a wet slump behind the bar. Then John turned to the crowd, most of whom were heavily armed, and said, "If you men want to play, you got to pay."

One drunken oaf from the wanted part of Oklahoma pulled a pistol out of his belt. John didn't wait to see if he were going to use it. He thumbed the hammers back on the scatter-gun and pulled the trigger. The pistol and most of the man's hand flew off into space. Some of the miners applied a tourniquet to stop the flow of blood. The man lived, but he pulled no more guns.

Then John said, "Is there one of you men in here that's got the guts to run this place? And stay cold sober while doing it?"

Oddly enough John had seven or eight volunteers. This episode might be called luck by many, but if it were, John's other experiences would prove him the luckiest man alive. Maybe it was something else.

The mines at Red River didn't last too long. Business went from good to fair and from fair to bad. John knew if he ever were to own the bridge, he would have to seek his wealth elsewhere.

John begged forgiveness for forgetting a few things at this point. He did it for his own protection, and for the protection of some of his friends, but he had plenty happen to him anyway. It is known, however, that before he wound up in Montana there had been the crack of many pistols, and the jangle of lots of gold coins.

John arrived in Billings broker than ever. It wasn't long until he had wind of something which sounded good. There was a big demand for deer meat in St. Paul and Minneapolis. But John realized it was a hopeless proposition unless he could persuade a railroad agent that there was money to be made.

This he did. Both of them agreed they could ship the venison as dressed sheep. John agreed to cut the agent in for one-third of all he took in. This may sound like poaching now, but at that time there were black-tail deer in that country by the tens of thousands.

It was no easy job. After the kill John had to skin and cut the deer. He used several pack horses and a couple of hired hands who were good skinners. At one time they shipped four hundred black-tails, and received twelve dollars and a half apiece for them. But this game soon got a little risky, and John decided to quit while he was still winner—a theory he followed for over ninety years.

He took a job as foreman of a big cow outfit that had a contract to deliver cattle to the Indian agency at Standing Rock, North Dakota. The contract called for one hundred and fifty thousand pounds of beef, or about two hundred and fifty head of small cows. John worked with a man by the name of McLaughlin. His son was the interpreter to the Sioux Indians.

They corraled the cattle at Standing Rock, where the Indians would kill them. Using horses and oxen, the Indians dragged the cattle onto an open flat, and butchered them. It was in these dealings that John was misled, like so many others, into believing that Sitting Bull, the historically famous chief, wasn't ranked too highly. The Bull's share of the beef was for only one hundred and twenty-five Indians, who were under his leadership, out of five thousand. Chief Gall and Chief Rain-in-the-Face appeared to be the big boys. They received the major share of the meat. The obvious was not quite true, however, and it only shows how history can become twisted in a short time by too many tellings. Sitting Bull had been put in charge of a lesser number of Indians by the government. This accounted for his getting the least amount of meat. But among his own people he was still the Big Chief, the greatest of them all.

While at Standing Rock John got what he considered was the authentic picture of the Custer Massacre. He was so interested in learning the facts that he worked around it, to the point that the interpreter brought a squaw to his tent. The interpreter told him she was noted for reliability, and would give John the real story for twenty dollars. John promptly handed over a twenty dollar gold piece.

The woman told him she had been in the battle because, as was the custom, she had taken her sick husband's place. The Sioux had been camped on the Little Big Horn, in a rocky, gully-marked, hogback. Custer camped three miles from what was later to be the battleground, and had been camped for several days. On the day of the battle, to a trumpet's blare, Custer and his men charged the Sioux camp, killing several Indians and wounding many more.

The Sioux retreated immediately across the Little Big Horn, into a rocky, gully-marked, hog-back. Custer and his men followed, falling neatly into the previously arranged trap. There was an Indian behind every rock, and the furious battle raged until, as most everyone knows, every soldier was killed. The squaw then related how she took part in the scalping of all except Custer. He was given the honor of keeping his hair because of his bravery.

The Sioux then retreated into Canada, where they surrendered to the Canadian government to be put on a reservation.

About this time John decided to increase his education. He had never been in a schoolhouse except to dance. So John hired a cowboy to teach him the alphabet. This cowboy had been through the fifth grade and, though he didn't know much else, John did get his ABC's. From this meager beginning John learned both to read and to write. In the years that followed he developed this smattering of knowledge until he could hold his own with the average man in any field. In fact, he was known to talk with the power of a statesman. Listeners were constantly amazed at his vocabulary, his wit, and his depth of thought.

John gained confidence after acquiring a little education, so he took once more to the gamblers' road. He dealt monte a while in Rapid City, then drifted on into Cheyenne. Because he was the only monte dealer there he really cleaned up. He could have saved enough then and there to buy his bridge, but life was a little fast, and expenses high in Cheyenne. It was at the peak of the great buffalo hunts, and hide money was coming in fast. The town was full of thieves from the hills, opium smugglers from Canada, and what seemed to him, whores by the million. There was at least one killing a day. John told of the time he was close to being one of them.

"One night a big poker game was a-roaring. I knew the man directly across the table from me was going to get killed. If I didn't kill him, one of the other three gamblers at the table would. At least somebody was sure going to some day.

"It all started that afternoon in a Cheyenne saloon. Now, I had been kicked around, one way or another, most of it my fault, for over forty years. But I was a little bit tired of it. This feller, named Pete something or other, had wound up saying he was the best roper, best rider, best fighter and best gambler in the whole damn world.

"Well, I was a fair hand myself with a rope, as a rider, and as a fighter. But when Pete mentioned gambling, that was a point I felt I could afford to brag a little myself. So, I worked it around into a poker game. Pete was plenty flush with money and whiskey. The bartender was doing his job all right, and if I had my way, he would do even better—with a cut out of my winnings.

"The game started fast. Pete high-played. That is, he raised and bluffed to beat hell. I sat back a while, and pitched in my draw. I waited for the opening I knew was bound to come. Pete was winning from the other boys, and he became noisier and dumber as he went along. Pretty soon, when he'd won a pot by a bluff, he couldn't keep from showing his hand to his opponent. I watched him close, and saw that when he was bluffing he invariably reached up and pulled at the brim of his hat.

"I dealt myself a spade flush, and Pete tried his big bluff. There was about sixteen hundred dollars in the pot when I took it. Pete turned red in the face, and made a remark under his breath. I didn't catch what it was he said, but I knew it wouldn't do to repeat at a Ladies' Aid meeting. Then the crazy fool started trying to stack the deck. He was as clumsy as a foundered mare. When it wasn't his deal he always called for a cut, and generally messed up the game worse than a red-feathered hen in a pile of fresh cow manure.

"Along about midnight the bartender called me aside and said, 'John, that fool is a trouble-maker. Watch him close.'

"I did. Next hand I was holding a full house, three aces, and a pair of sixes. I had him over a barrel. The wise guy had a good hand, and bet his pile. The pot had over six thousand dollars in it. He turned over a ten-high straight. It looked pale and sick beside my full house. Pete looked that way, too.

"Then he said, 'You cheatin' dog,' and pulled at his side-arm.

"The bartender saved my life right then by slamming Pete across the arm with a piece of stove wood.

"I leaped up and grabbed the stove wood from the bartender, and laid it nice and hard along the line of Pete's jaw, below the left ear. It popped, and Pete fell about ten feet. He didn't even wiggle a toe for about thirty minutes, and when he came around the bartender pointed at the door and he hit it fast. One reason for his hasty departure was that the bartender was

waving a buffalo gun—first at him, then to the door.
We resumed the game in peace and quiet."

John believes that Cheyenne was the best gambling
town he was ever in. It may have been due to the fact
that several regiments of Negro soldiers were camped
nearby. John made money like a mint but spent it just
as fast—too many temptations in Cheyenne.

An opportunity came to him to join a troupe of gamblers who traveled with a carnival. He took it. They
made a stop-over at Santa Barbara, California, where
they were having a big town doings. John heard about
their steer-roping contest. He entered, and took all the
bets he could get on himself. The cowboys figured he
was only a tin-horn gambler, so they readily took up
his bets.

At this event John had to rope on a rented horse, and
what made it so hard was that this horse had only been
used in dally country, where they simply wrap the rope
around the saddle horn. John tied hard and fast. The
horse's owner raised hell when he found that out.
"You'll ruin my horse," he moaned.

John didn't want any trouble with him, but he was
the first man to rope, and the cowboys wanted to get
started. Another thing—John already had bet all his
money. So, as one of the spectators later told: "He
walked over to this fellow, and knocked him as cold as
a piss-ant in a blizzard."

The dally men used extra long rawhide ropes, while John used a short hemp. John had worked so much in brush country that he had learned to catch quickly in a small opening, where a long rope was useless. Consequently that old long arm of his dropped the rope over the steer's head before he'd hardly started.

The steer hit the end of the rope with such force that he went up and came down with a terrific impact on his head. He hit so hard that one horn was broken, and many spectators claimed it sailed into the air as high as the city jail. John tied the steer in one of the fastest times known at that date.

John made a fair winning from the roping match, but it was still a long way from fifteen thousand dollars, and that's what he must have to buy the bridge.

While the gambling troupe was enroute from Marysville to Sausalito, California, John hatched another scheme that had a chance of paying off. He slipped into the car that carried all the gambling equipment, and quickly jimmied a roulette wheel so that it would fall on certain numbers. The next night he played roulette against his own troupe and won seven thousand dollars.

With that, John suddenly felt the urge to breathe fresher air afar—a far distance from the carnival.

His next stop turned out to be Goldfield, Nevada, which was going through a tremendous mining boom. Twenty thousand people were jammed into its small confines. It seemed that all the people from the recent Klondike boom were there, including the gamblers and their sweethearts.

The hills were filled with miners, working their dry-washers in the dry creeks, and gold pans where they could find a little water. Shaking and looking, hour upon dragging hour, some finding, others hoping, but everybody trying for the golden dream in one way or another.

The big companies moved in and set up mills, while the small miners dug into the hard-rock veins by holding a sharpened steel about eighteen inches long in one hand (this has been called a "bull prick" by miners since the beginning of time) and in the other hand they swung a "single Jack." This was a sledge hammer light enough to be handled with one arm. It was slow work, hard, body-jarring work. When a hole had finally been pounded deep enough it was loaded with powder, and BOOM she went. It was what each round of blasting would reveal that kept them going. The very next might expose riches untold! No wonder it was wild and woolly in town when the miners came to celebrate and spend their golden earnings, or to look for a grubstake when the veins had petered out.

This was not why John was here, however. He was there because the money was there. When he wasn't thinking of how to get somebody else's gold and silver over into his pocket, his mind was back in Taos on that big dream—the dream he meant to fulfill right here, where the money was almost free for the taking, and the men and women willing.

In his old age, John spoke of this—gritting his teeth, remembering his own forceful determination. "By doggies, I wasn't waiting any longer. I was going to get it right here, unless everybody in Nevada went to the poorhouse. And if they did I was going to set up a roulette wheel right on the bread-line!" Then he into a spasm of laughing, and talked high and shrilly through that long mutilated nose of his.

"They were all drunk, except me, and I couldn't get a job because I was sober."

This didn't stop John for long. He promptly opened up a place of his own, calling it the Alamo. It was still there, under the same name, just a few years back.

Here John had one of his very few streaks of bad luck, and went broke the first night. A man by the name of Tex Rickard had a place next door, and offered him a job at twenty-five dollars a shift. John replied in kind,

"You don't think that a man of my ability would risk my life at your gaming table for that sum, do you?"

Rickard understood, and told him to take out what he figured he was worth after each shift. John worked two shifts a day, totaling sixteen hours, and after each shift he pocketed a hundred dollars. John expected Rickard to fire him the first night, but considering that he won two or three thousand a night, Rickard's leni-

ency can well be understood. It wasn't long before John
opened up his own place again.

John picked up an old acquaintance he'd made in
Mexico. The man was a good cook and housekeeper.
John told him if he would do that part of the job, he
would make him a partner. This old boy John called
Sowbelly, and Sowbelly readily accepted. Life began
to take on a different glow. They had their beds and
kitchen in the back of the place, and gambling and saloon business in the front.

Goldfield people were absolutely mad to gamble.
It didn't bother them at all to lose. If they won, it wasn't
but a few hours until they were back gambling again.
Everybody had money, and if they didn't they could
soon get it. When people get in a big boom of any kind,
they lose all sense of balance.

John remembers it as being something like a fever.
"The women were wilder than outhouse rats, and I'm
pretty sure they wound up with all the money the gamblers didn't get. Anyway, I was glad to be there, because I won steadily, and my bankroll grew fatter fast.
I already had about a fourth of the transportation
money stashed away.

"A painted woman by the name of Dora called me
aside one night, and put a proposition to me. She said
she was sleeping with a mine owner who had made a
big strike. She wanted to act as a shill, to steer him into
a game at my table. She, of course, was asking a price,

and the price was a fifty-fifty split. I cut her down to a third, and the deal was on.

"She started out like I've seen it done a thousand times, by getting her man drunk. It didn't take long, even though we were serving watered-down whiskey. He lost rapidly. Dora, with the mine owner's money, played and, of course, lost heavily.

"Later, after she had put him to bed in a passed out condition, she came back for her cut. I gave it to her, and thought to myself that the mine owner had paid a hell of a high price for a bed partner."

A little-known event that took place through the promotional abilities of the famous Tex Rickard was a matched fight between John and a huge miner by the name of Clive.

Clive would come to town, wham his gold poke on a bar top, and buy drinks for the house. As soon as he figured the other patrons were drunk enough, he'd challenge them one at a time to a fist fight. He always won. He fought like a bull, head down, big arms and fists flailing in wide powerful arcs. It soon got so that no one would take him on.

One day after he had made a big killing in the mines he offered to bet any man that he could whip him in five minutes. The sum he offered was twenty thousand dollars. Tex Rickard had witnessed John dispose of several customers who had become loud and resentful.

This had been done with such speed that he offered to call the man's bet.

John agreed to the fight, when Rickard told him he would give him half if he won. Neither John nor Rickard believed that John could whip Clive, but they both figured he could out-dodge him for five minutes. The fight was to be held behind John's place, in Goldfield. Word got around, and spectators were quickly on hand to see and to make bets. Rickard bet several thousand more on the side.

John had done some figuring in the meantime. He borrowed his partner's watch, and set it up so that it ran double fast. It was arranged by Rickard that this was to be the watch used to time the fight, although Rickard didn't actually know what John had done to it.

Clive lunged at John, swinging wildly. John neatly sidestepped each charge, until one of the miners who had bet on Clive stuck his foot under John. John went down, but before Clive could get at him several of the men who had bet on John leaped at the tripper. Clive became so mad at this interruption that he started bashing away at any and everyone in his reach. He scattered men about like broken sticks.

All this time John managed to keep out of the fight, and although his five minutes had already swept by on the watch, he knew Clive was tiring. He stepped up beside him, and hit him behind the ear. Clive went down, but before he could get up John lashed out with one of his long boot-encased legs. It caught Clive in the pit of the stomach and all the air was knocked out of him. He rolled over and over on the ground, moaning.

John, realizing that they still had to collect the bets, ran inside and came back out with his ever faithful shotgun. He fired a couple of rounds over the heads of the brawlers and, by the time they quieted down, he had reloaded and was issuing orders as to the payments of bets. Rickard, no mean hand at getting money in his palms, really cleaned up.

Clive took it pretty well. He said, "It was almost worth the money I lost just to be in a hell-bustin' free-for-all like that."

It had been a big night—especially big because of Clive's lost money. After John locked up, he headed for the back room to count up his total winnings from Clive and the double-crossing woman a few days before. Forty-two thousand, clear money.

"Right then a chill went all over me," John related. "I looked over at my partner, Sowbelly, and saw that he was in deep sleep. I sacked the money then and there, got my horse out of the stables, and left town. I neglected to mention this to my partner, but I don't think he minded. After all, I had left him a thriving saloon business, and he hadn't put up a dime. Besides that, he was sleeping so good I just couldn't stand to wake him up to say goodbye."

There was a vision before John's eyes. He was headed for Taos again, and his bridge. He had forty-two thousand in cash, and he swore that no gambling son-of-a-bitch was going to take it away from him.

X

The first night back in Taos, John met Meyers, the owner of the bridge. They were both staying at the old Don Fernando Hotel. John said nothing about the bridge until next day. He saw Meyers crossing the plaza, so he rode over to him.

"Meyers," John said, "I know a man who might buy your bridge. That is, if you're interested."

"Yes, I do wanna sell. But I don't wanna talk to a man with no money."

"What's your price?"

"Twenty-two hundred. Cash."

"Twenty-two hundred," John repeated. "Well, I might find just the man you want. Would it be worth a hundred to you for me to swing the deal?"

"A hundred is yours—if you sell it."

Meyers walked away, and John just stood there and gazed unbelievingly after him. Fifteen thousand dollars was tucked neatly in his shirt front. It was such a change in price from his first offer that John very nearly fell dead.

That night they met again in the Don Fernando. When John handed over the cash for the bridge, it was Meyer's turn to nearly fall dead. He counted the money and handed John his hundred dollars commission. When he wrote out the bill of sale he asked, "What name?" John told him, "John Dunn," and then added, "I thought it was such a bargain, I just sold it to myself."

John walked out on air, happy to the extreme in just thinking that at last he had realized his only sought-after wish. His happiness was short lived, however. John quickly learned that the reason the bridge had sold so cheaply was that competition was setting in. Two Taos merchants, Albert Miller and Gerson Gusdorf were putting in a bridge at Mambe Springs. All three principals had great respect for one another—at least enough that, after some discussion, it was agreed to sell their bridge to John for fifteen hundred.

Now John was set, at least for a while. As hoped, his toll bridge business went over big. John made over two hundred and fifty dollars a day at the bridge. He charged a dollar a person, fifty cents apiece for horses and cattle, and twenty-five cents a head for sheep.

Sometimes a few reneged from paying that steep toll fee. They were hardly sympathetic to the long struggle John had been through to acquire his bridge. However, they were quickly goaded into reaching for their purses by the simple act of getting a good close peek at the inside of a shotgun barrel. That always did make people mighty agreeable to John.

Now everybody around Taos looked up to John, and talked about him constantly. His very personal appearance was enough, without his force and cunning—six-feet-four straight from the ground to his mustached face, strong blue eyes with a twinkle of devilment in them. For there was a lot of the devil in John. One striking feature about him was his ears. They were long and pointed. His nose was long. His hands were extra long. He had a long waxed mustache which was his only vanity. He kept it waxed even on a snowy day. Truly John lived up to that long part of his name. He was long in every way, including brains.

When he stood in a crowd it was not only his great height that was impressive, but the straightness of his bearing, and the *sureness* about him. As one of his old friends remarked, "Hell, you couldn't miss old John. He stood out among humans like a whore in church. When he stood behind a big stack of silver at one of his gambling places he made you feel like it was almost a privilege to lose your money to him, and he'd always make you laugh, even if you didn't want to."

Business at the bridge continued to be good. John was feeling fine—mighty fine, but just as he was breathing free and easy, a chinook wind rolled in from Colorado, prematurely melting the snow in the mountains, and was followed by heavy rains. The water rose six feet higher than at any time in history and washed out both of John's bridges. It was a disastrous blow, but he had fought this battle too long to give up now.

John rounded up as much help as he could get and went to work rebuilding his big bridge. It wasn't easy. Logs had to be hauled for miles, but they got them to Arroyo Hondo. John later told John E. Miles, the governor of New Mexico, "Thank God we didn't have a National Forest then, otherwise I would never have been able to rebuild my bridge. Nowadays, a man can't cut a log or take a drink of water without getting permission."

They saved several miles and lots of hours by rolling the logs off the top of the gorge just north of Hondo Canyon. They didn't have to worry about hauling rocks. They had plenty all around them for the gathering. After acquiring enough material to start the actual construction, John said, "Boys, now there's got to be a cable swung across to the other side of the Rio Grande before we can do a damn thing."

The boys didn't say a word; not one.

So John said, "When we were talking about this, back in the Hondo Forest, you fellers all barked like a bunch of half-breed water spaniels—but now, it looks like you never had a drink of water in your lives and don't ever want any."

There was only one thing left to do and that was swim across himself. John did. The water was still rolling fast. It was a little muddy, and plenty cold, but that cable was put across the treacherous Rio Grande.

The work went on from there pretty fast, and John soon had a good, substantial bridge completed.

It was right after this that John decided Taos was a place for tourists and people of finer tastes to visit and live. He had heard from Sharp and Phillips, two of the pioneer artists, that there was no place on earth that offered so great a variety of scenery to see and paint.

Taos sits in a valley to the west of what D. H. Lawrence the world-famed British writer who made Taos his home called "the most dramatic skyline in the world," the Sangre de Cristos (Blood of Christ) Mountains. In the winter their tall slopes are white with many feet of snow. In the spring this snow melts and pours down trout-filled streams into the Rio Grande River several miles to the east. Many of the streams course through Taos, and fishing can be had right on graded roads.

Taos is really several little settlements in one long fertile valley. Ranchos de Taos to the south four miles, is famous for its old Spanish Mission Church, said to be painted more times by artists than any other building in the world with possible exception of the Taj Mahal in India. To the north are Arroyo Hondo and Arroyo Seco. Most of the homes are built of mud, and are mud plastered. Their low flat-roofed profiles blend into the earth, as though they had sprung right out of the ground. The ancient Indian pueblo, housing over one thousand Indians, lies only two miles to the north and east of Taos.

When John came back to Taos the second time, he found the plaza lined with wagons, horses and buggies. The Spanish farmers and sheepmen came to town to trade and gossip, and the Indians did likewise. It was an oddity to see the three races, including the Anglo, mixing together so peacefully after so much bloodshed in the past.

John was a man who liked to dance, and he also liked to mix with the fair sex. As his business made more and more money he would often hire Spanish musicians and throw a big *baile*. His long legs would flash all night and everyone had a big time. John gained much in popularity for this. His dances were usually peaceful because he would usually tell his guests, "Now we came here to dance, and have fun. If you wanta fight, get started now, so you won't bother the musicians later."

In those days the desert to the west, toward and on beyond the Rio Grande Gorge, was covered with an abundance of good grass, and scattered about was some sagebrush. More and more the sheepmen from the mountains came down to winter on this land. These natural pastures were soon overstocked, and gradually the earth was overtaken by sagebrush. What was lost in pasture land was made up, in a way, by the beauty of the sage. It glows a soft green at midday, but near sundown it shows various shades of violet and deep blues. Artists have covered canvas after canvas with paintings of this plant in its many moods and colors.

The Sangre de Cristos got their name from the beautiful red color that spreads out over their enormous slopes in the late afternoon. In the summer the green overtakes the whole range. The aspen, the pine, and the spruce wave in the soft breezes. Wild game, deer, bear, beaver and many other wild creatures make their different ways through their slopes.

In the fall the aspens turn to deep gold and bright yellow. Painters and tourists flock to them for rest and inspiration. The artists, long noted as being in a profession of little financial reward, soon learned that there was a ready market for pictures of such colorful trees. It was a combination of all these things that convinced John Dunn that Taos could be one of the show spots of the world.

That is when he took upon himself, a wanted man, to risk going to Denver to see the railroad's general passenger agent about building a line from Taos Junction to Servietta. The gentleman in Denver had never heard of Long John Dunn, but was so impressed by his bearing that he gave him a hearing.

When it was over the man was so firm a believer in the possibilities of the Taos area, that he threw all his influence and knowledge into the project. It wasn't long until the action was taken, for which Long John was directly responsible. This gave Taos the boost it needed, and did much to add to its world-wide attraction.

XI

Wᴴᴇɴ the railroad line was
built to Servietta, Taos received lots of advertisement.
Soon John had all the business he could take care of,
and was hauling passengers from Taos Junction, too.

These were the busiest years of his life. John had the
toll bridge, several stages, and teams of good horses.
He built a hotel, or what he called a "road ranch" at
the mouth of Hondo Canyon, where the Rio Hondo
empties into the Rio Grande. John declared, proudly,
"It looked like a castle setting up there against those
rocky bluffs." He always delayed his last stagecoach
so the passengers would have to stay all night in this
fine road-ranch. "It was really too much of a haul to
make the trip in one day, anyway," John said. They
were given clean rooms, and John fed them well. He

kept a Mexican around who did nothing but fish, and he was a good fisherman. Nearly always there was fresh trout for the guests. The road-ranch had its own milk cows, and good stables for the horses.

Profits mounted. There was no doubt that Long John was the "goin'est feller" in the Land of Mañana at the time—getting more done, and making more money, than fifty average men.

John was able to send for his aging mother, and she stayed at Hondo with him for several years. Soon after that she went out to California for her health. She died in California, but John felt she was happy at the end.

But the stage business had some drawbacks. In winters the steep winding road in and out of Hondo was really slick. Besides being very steep, the road was bordered on one edge by the deep rocky gorge carved for centuries by the Rio Grande River. John had plenty of his passengers faint. In the spring, when the thaw came, big boulders would roll into the road. John always carried a bundle of dynamite along in case the rocks were too big to roll out of the way by hand. There wasn't an oil road in the country in those days. Men built their roads and bridges as they came to them.

Once a pregnant woman asked John what he thought this ride would do to her. For a moment John was stopped, but since he was a plain-spoken man, and always tried to answer passengers' questions, he said, "I don't know, Ma'am, I've never been in your condition."

John related, "She was indignant at this," and he laughed. "She ruffled up like a hen in a summer shower, and said if she had a step-ladder, she'd slap my face.

"Another time," John continued, "a big, fat feller leaned out and looked down several hundred feet to the bottom of the rocky gorge, and asked, 'Say, driver, does a stage fall off this road very often?' "

" 'No, only once,' I answered. The heavy man shut up the rest of the trip."

J. Frank Dobie, the famous western writer, quoted John in one of his newspaper columns: "John Dunn will long be remembered as one of the characters of Taos, N. M. He used to run a stage over the mountain road to Taos Junction and back. On this route he drove the first automobile of the country. One time he took on three passengers at the Junction—two men and a woman. The woman riding in front, exclaimed at the scenery, ejaculated at the perilous brinks along the road, asked questions and chattered all the way. When the journey ended, the men descended with alacrity.

"How much?" one asked.

"Two and a half," Dunn replied.

He paid.

"Can you change a five?" the second asked.

"Here's your change."

"What did you say the fare was?" the woman now chirped, offering a bill.

"Five dollars."

"Why, Mr. Dunn, I just heard you tell those men it was two and a half," she protested.

"Madam, they did not talk."

"And John Dunn kept the talker's five dollars."

John had four saloons in town, and a gambling hall, as well as the livery business. As the business at John Dunn's bridge prospered, his roulette wheels in town were a source of considerable income. Most gambling was done in the old Don Fernando Hotel, established by that well-known pioneer merchant, Gerson Gusdorf. Here John met many personages of the day. Will Rogers and Vice President Dawes made a special trip to see him. Rogers had heard so much about John's native humor he wanted to meet one of his own kind. John felt highly honored.

Up Twining Canyon, about seventeen miles north of Taos, a mining boom was under way. The Taos Mining Company claimed in their brochure, mailed out as a public offering to sell stock, "We aim to supply the world with copper!"

Indeed they did have lots of copper, gold and silver, according to the reports written by some prominent geologists of the time. Mr. Ira M. Gilman said in his report, written in 1895, that he estimated a total of 3,880,000 tons. This large quantity of ore could be taken out without the use of hoisting machinery. On Vein No. 2, with hundreds of thousands of tons in sight, he estimated the values per ton to be gold $10.33,

Long John Dunn unloading baggage at Taos from his mechanical stage coach in 1927.

John Dunn and the first car he used to come up the Rio Grande Gorge Trail to Taos. He made the trail, with his horse-drawn stagecoach.

silver 8½ ounces, copper 6 percent. The other two major veins were estimated to be the equivalent.

C. L. Henrick, consulting geologist from the University of New Mexico, gave an analysis from Pueblo Smelter, across a one hundred and fifty foot vein, as $22.20 per ton, with gold at twenty dollars an ounce, and copper at eight cents. He added that, "In location, position and outside resources the properties were all that could be desired."

Other geologists were just as enthusiastic in their reports, so it is little wonder that a town was started which included a large mill and smelter, bars and hotels. Excitement ran high.

John went up there and lost no time in taking over the gambling. He later said, "The miners' money went through their hands into mine, like salts through a windy woman."

Things didn't turn out so well for the others. The bottom suddenly dropped out from under copper, and it went as low as four cents a pound. Dissension set in, and trouble started among the organizers and principals, which included William Frazer, who has the mountain where the tunnels are driven named in his honor; Frank Cheetham, Esq., counsellor at law and U. S. District Court Commissioner; Honorable Alexander Gusdorf, fruit and stock grower; Honorable W. G. Sargent, the mayor of Santa Fe; A. M. Richardson, cashier of the First National Bank of Taos; A. C. Probert, M.D.; H. F. Probert, M.E.; Harry W. Davis, Vice President and Secretary of Delaware Trust Co.; and many others.

A lot of fighting and strange disappearances took place. A key to this might be found in geological reports of November, 1909, by F. W. Traphagen, Ph.D. (London) which stated: "The main vein averages from ten feet to as much as seventy feet and in places is very rich. From an open cut, Mr. Frazer took out ore yielding him six thousand dollars in an *arrastra*—six thousand dollars in gold!" An *arrastra* is a stone, tank-like affair. In the middle is a pole with a heavy, hard rock tied on the end. A horse is tied to the other end, and pulls it around and around to grind the ore. As the ore is crushed the heavier particles of gold and other metals settle to the bottom, where they can later be recovered. Mr. L. A. Jones of Questa, New Mexico, still has this old *arrastra* rock, and a streak of pure gold is plainly visible across its face.

Evidently Mr. Frazer had found something the others hadn't. It finally ended with Probert shooting Fraser; killing him in front of his cabin at the forks of the Lake Fork Creek and Arroyo Hondo. Tom Holder, the man who saved John's life by hiding him under a load of hay at the Texas border, and his son, Tom Holder, Jr., were standing behind Frazer when Probert fired. The bullet passed through Frazer's body and into the spine of Tom Holder, Jr. It remains there to this day. Tom Holder, Jr. is a noted game warden now in the Taos area.

This just about wound up the mining boom. The mines went into the hands of the receivers. By then John already had packed up and left. He said, somewhat regretfully for him, "I think the ore was there all right, it was just the wrong time to take it out. I'm the only one that left there showing a sizable profit as far as I know."

On top of all these other things, John applied for a mail route, which included Taos Junction, Embudo and Servietta. One of his helpers was Edwin Hart of Ranchos de Taos. They carried the mail in buckboards.

Much of the parcel post included paintings being sent in and out by famous pioneer Taos artists. Paint, paint brushes, canvas and picture frames arrived from Chicago, New York and Boston. While a great percentage of first class mail was received, there was always a lot of winter mail to be forwarded to artists away for the season. This proved pretty good going for a man wanted by the law in several western and adjoining states.

To John's knowledge, Joseph H. Sharp was the first artist in Taos. He came a couple of years before John did. Bert Phillips and Blumenschien came in from Denver with a hack and team. Bert Phillips was the first one to come and stay permanently. Then other artists began hearing about the colorful Taos country.

John Young-Hunter, Ward Lockwood, O. E. Berninghaus, Charles Berninghaus, Walter Ufer, Andrew Dasburg, Joe Fleck, Victor Higgins, Buck Dunton and others soon followed. Among the many writers who were to make their homes in Taos were, Frank Waters, Victor White, Joseph Foster, Frances Crane, Frank O'Rourke—and of course D. H. Lawrence.

After John had advertised fully, and gotten them coming, he hauled all the artists and other people coming to Taos until 1930. Here are those whom John believed made Taos: "The artists, first and foremost, because they advertised Taos across the Atlantic and across the Pacific and in between the two oceans. They never made a complaint about all the hardships, and they had many. I'm satisfied they're the easiest bunch of people to get along with it has ever been my privilege to meet.

"Writer Mabel Dodge Lujan contributed a great deal to the poor people of Taos. She gave us the hospital, bandstand, and many other things. Mabel is one of the finest persons I've ever known.

"Next on the list is John Harris Dunn. I hauled 'em in, and I took care of 'em on the way. Finally there's that fine man and merchant, Gerson Gusdorf. He took care of 'em after they arrived."

John, with his position as the man in control of all gambling in Northern New Mexico, the man who brought the travelers in and brought them safely—except for their gambling dollars—the man who never backed down, and figured no man his superior and damn few his equal, was sought after at many social functions. If he liked the people who invited him he went. If he didn't he stayed away.

He attended anything Mabel Dodge asked him to, and there is little doubt that she felt great pride in his tall, almost arrogant figure, with his direct, salty, nasal-whanging tales to entertain her friends from all parts of the world.

Now, one thing John never failed to do, was pull out his long bladed knife, which he called "Old Barlow," when the meat was served. He kept the blade as sharp as a whetstone could make it. He never used any other knife for over forty years. "I never saw a silver knife in a home or a restaurant that would cut through wet sawdust, much less a chunk of good tough meat," he said with conviction. When he wasn't eating or talking, he eternally kept a fine cigar puffing away. And there was no question about his great delight in a really good cigar.

John must have established some kind of record as a stagedriver. He was never over five minutes late on any run, even though his line ran the mountain country to E-Town and Ute Park in sometimes near-blizzard weather. Nor was anyone ever robbed, killed or injured in any way while under his care. This is astonishing, when it is considered how many road bandits there were operating in that day. That old scatter-gun of John's might have had something to do with it.

An interesting thing occurred in the beautiful mountains thirty miles north of Taos. There in a valley lay a little town called Red River, and it was rapidly becoming a resort spot. It had settled itself down in some of the most gorgeous country on earth. Somehow, no one had taken the trouble to get a clear title to the place. Of course, a man couldn't get away with anything like this nowadays, but in those days the property belonged to a man strong enough to take it and keep it. In this case, that man was Long John Dunn. In doing it, John just about outshone all the old-time gunmen. It's doubtful if any of them, single handed, ever took over a town so completely and in such a short time as did Long John.

One fine spring day John rode a good-looking sorrel gelding up to Red River. He had a .45 pistol, a .30-.30 rifle, and a double barreled shotgun as his saddle partners. With these he took possession. There were some who disagreed with the procedures, but John was still in the bounds of the law, and he figured he was as good or a better shot than any of them. His tall, straight figure, with its cold, certain, laughing eyes and his reputation as a dead-shot helped put it across.

It was, of course, at the risk of his life that he hung on. It was bold and risky business for any man to try taking over a whole town by himself. He later explained, "I expected all the time to look down and see where a .30-.30 bullet had punched a hole in my shirt on its way out of my skinny frame."

John seldom asked for a fight, and always resorted to cunning if possible to save bloodshed, but when the occasion arose to get risky, he was in there with the best that ever lived in the west.

Most of the residents by this time had heard about John and his shotgun, and had decided to keep hands off. Few men wanted any trouble with him. He was not one to "take crap from anybody," and he had that force about him that made most men careful and cautious, and wisely so.

There were four men, however, who foolishly resented his entrance and his taking-over Red River. They decided to ambush John. John got word of this through a Mexican friend of his. He understood they were holed up in an old vacant saloon. It so happened that this was the saloon John once had owned.

The night after learning about the plans of the four men, John made some plans of his own. He loaded several shotgun shells with salt, after removing the buckshot. He slipped quietly up to the back door of the saloon, and poured a can of turpentine on the floor. He could hear the men talking, and knew they were heavily armed. Then he struck a match to the turpentine.

John ran around to the front of the building and waited. Pretty soon he heard one yell, "The damned

building is on fire!" All four piled out the front door.
John waited till they were outside, and then cut down
on them with the shotgun.

The men piled up, screaming—thinking for sure
they had been blown to pieces. Then they ran like
scalded cats. The salt had set them on fire almost as
much as the saloon building. Their wounds did them
no permanent harm physically but John was no longer
worried with their presence in Red River. The saloon
burned to the ground, but John hung on until his title
was cleared.

Then and there John owned a whole town, lock,
stock and roulette wheel. It had cost him only a few
hundred dollars for the title. He later disposed of it
for thousands. One of the buyers was a Mr. Simion. His
son Tony still owns and operates a business there.

Once a man asked John how many times he had
been married. John said, "Ten times in this high alti-
tude." No one ever thought to ask him about the lower
elevations.

In those days there was very little divorce. If a couple got to squabbling the man would split the blanket,
sack up and leave. Even in his old age John unhesitat-
ingly did it when he thought the going too rough.

There was one time, however, when John really got
"took," so to speak, by a redhead called Peachy. Her
brother, a tinhorn gambler, had stopped over in Taos
for a visit. He got in a monte game with John. Once

when John was paying him off thirty dollars, his long fingers retained twenty of it. The tinhorn caught him at it, but while he was turned to an observer to brag about catching John, John lifted forty more dollars off the tinhorn's stack.

When the game was over the tinhorn was broke, and in spite of John loaning him money to get out of town, he harbored a grudge.

It was only a short time after this that a beautiful red-headed woman came to town. She asked where she might rent a buggy to see the country. Of course, she was referred to Long John.

He hitched the team up himself, and they rode about with John bragging to beat hell on the Taos country. It was love at first sight for John, and hardly three days had passed before he had proposed. At first, the redhead was reluctant, then finally at John's continued insistence she gave in.

John was the happiest man in the world. He told everybody about his conquest, and prepared to have a big wedding with all the trimmings. But before the nuptial affair could take place a wire came in from California. It seems that Peachy's mother was seriously ill, and the redhead was needed at her dying side. She told John about this, saying, "I don't know what to do. I don't have enough money to make the trip."

John consoled her immediately, "Now, honey, don't you worry none. Here's two thousand." He loaded her in the buggy and drove her to Servietta to catch the train. The narrow gauge railroad train was hours late. All this time the redhead kept telling John how she hated to use his money this way. And John said, "Now, don't you worry your pretty head, it's all in the family now, anyway. At least it soon will be."

He kept looking at her, and repeatedly telling Phil Dickman, the agent, "Ain't she a peach, Phil?"

At long last she caught the train. Days later John received another wire saying that Peachy's mother had died, and she would need a thousand for burial expenses. John sent the money right along. He figured it would speed her return.

Then she wired for five hundred to return to Taos and her true love. This, too, was duly sent. John waited day and night for two weeks for her return, but she never showed up.

It turned out later that it was the tinhorn's sister. He had gotten his revenge—and his money back. It was one of the rare times John was ever beaten, and stayed beaten.

Just before the auto came to prominence, John met a pretty little Spanish girl. Adelaide was her name. She captured his heart by refusing to ride inside the coach, but insisted on riding in the driver's seat with John. She was a pretty little thing, and several years younger than John.

John married Adelaide, and their marriage was fruitful. Born to them were four girls, Edith, Ella, Helene
and Susan, in that order. They all grew up into fine-
looking women, and are successfully married today.

In 1922, an influenza epidemic hit Taos, and babies
were dying like flies. John sent his wife and daughters
to Venice, California, until it was over. While there,
at Venice, Adelaide entered Edith in a baby contest
against over two thousand entries. John was proud to
say that she won hands down. Years later Helene was
chosen as queen of the Santa Fe fiesta, and that is always an honor to be coveted.

There was also a boy born to them. He was named
John Dunn, Jr. They lost him after only eleven years
of his life. This was the hardest blow of John's life. He
had wanted and planned that the boy would grow up
in his image—with these exceptions: He didn't want
him to have to sleep in the brush like a wild wolf as he
had done for so many years; he didn't want him to have
to ride for months looking back over his shoulder, and
expecting any minute to have a .30-.30 bullet knock
his heart out. Most of all, though, he didn't want him to
turn into a gambler.

Though gambling was a prosperous business for
John, he declared emphatically, "Sure, but there were
and are today thousands to my one who've died a pauper's death. Most are would-be gamblers, and even if

they are fortunate enough to make an occasional winning, think of the times that they go without.

"It gets into a man's blood so he won't work at anything else. Many a gambler has been shot from under the table trying to be crooked with fingers that just weren't fast enough. The hours are long and man-killing. I've seen men play for days and nights with nothing to eat, and nothing to drink but whiskey. Whiskey has pushed more gambling money across the table to sober men than all the dumb players on earth." That's the reason John always stayed sober.

He had put his whole heart into the rearing of John, Jr. The boy was with John almost constantly. John wanted his boy to have every chance that had been denied him, and without interference—but it was not intended that way.

When John was over eighty years old, and the boy was eleven, the doctors discovered the lad had an incurable disease of the kidneys. Reluctantly John accepted the tragic decree, but was still hopeful there might be one man who could cure his son. With this hope in mind, he traveled with the boy thousands of miles, and spent many thousands of dollars. Before he was through, he had spent his entire fortune. Eighty years of hardship went to save his son. In spite of everything the boy died.

It was a low blow, and no one could call an eighty-year-old man a kid. Everyone said John was too old to make a comeback. Well, he always *was* bull-headed when people told him he couldn't do a thing, especially if he wanted to do it.

XII

JOHN borrowed nine hundred dollars from a friend. He knew he was too old to play long-drawn-out games. He picked, for his play, only successful gamblers who had made big winnings on their own. Quickly he transferred their winnings to his own pocket. John made the comeback, all right. But for a long time after John Dunn, Jr. was gone the winnings had a hollow ring.

With the advent of the automobile John's life changed immeasurably. For him it was a hard change to make. All those years he had spent in the saddle and in the buckboard seat had created in his heart a great partiality for the horse.

Reports had been filtering in from the east about Mr. Ford's contraption quite a while before John could make up his mind to try the change-over from horse-drawn transportation to the mechanical. The horse was a living creature. John could talk to a horse when lonesome. He could work him when in need and curse him when angered. Besides, his life had been saved over and over by the swift departure into the forest and badlands on the back of the faithful horse.

John talked to Mace MacHorse, who had just put in the first Ford agency in the Taos area. Mace Mac-Horse, like John, had received a request to pull stakes after the law found out about him limbering up his rope. They didn't mind him dragging his rope along behind his saddle horse to get the kinks out so much, but they resented the fat calf that had stuck its head into the loop. And they especially felt bad about the calf having another man's brand on it. MacHorse migrated to Roswell, where he worked in a livery stable for a while, and on the old Flying H Ranch. He then moved over to Taos and put in the agency.

MacHorse was then, and still is, a smooth talker, and it wasn't long until he had John sold on the idea of a Ford. It was the first Ford sold in Taos. The first year MacHorse sold five Fords. He wrote the Ford Motor Company to tell them they had better kick up production. He thought he had sold every car they had made that year.

Now, MacHorse was one of, if not John's best friend. It is understandable, in that they both left Texas under

John Dunn looks at his bridge, spanning the Rio Grande, 1000 miles
above the Gulf of Mexico.

The Dunn home in Taos, New Mexico. The aged John, in the last year of his life, in the foreground.

similar conditions, and came from adjoining counties in that state—Comanche and Brown.

MacHorse went over for a little visit to Leavenworth at the invitation of Federal Judge Neblitt in 1929 and 1930. He says he was sent up "Because I was taking a little too much interest in the government's business." Someone had accused Mace of bootlegging. A lot of people still think Mace took the rap for someone else who deserved it more than he did. He told the Judge "I'll go, but I'll never take nobody with me."

When he returned to Taos, Long John Dunn put him right back into the car business, without asking for security of any kind. Mace says about John: "Yeah, he was a rough old customer, smooth and polished as glass. Smarter than a sure-enough smart fox, and tougher than a bay mule."

Mace tells this story about John: "I was standing watching John gamble with a bunch of oil men in the early thirties. Now, John had the longest fingers and hands of any man I ever saw, and they were limber and lightning fast. But one of these oil operators was plenty sharp-eyed, and he caught old John palming about a third of the chips when he was paying off.

The oil man yelled for all his friends to hear, "Hey, John, you shorted me."

John just grinned, and snapped back through his nose. "Excuse me, friend, you can't blame a hungry boy for trying."

The oil man turned to tell his buddies, "See there, I caught the old S.O.B."

While his head was turned for that fraction of a minute, John palmed five ten dollar chips. The oil man went on losing, all the time satisfied he was the sharpest gambler in the west.

"One thing about old John that was on the good side," says Mace, "he never let a kid gamble at one of his tables. He said there were enough grown up fools to work on anyhow. Another thing, he would always let a broke man have a few dollars, too. But just let a bunch of miners hit town, like back in 1920 to '25, when the molybdenum mines were booming north of Taos, and old John was there playing, laughing, joking, palming chips, dealing every way but the right way, and if need be doing a little head-clonking on the side till he had a lot of silver to match those stacks he used to lure the suckers into the trap."

One thing about Mace that amused John was the time he divorced his Indian wife. It's a matter of record in the Taos County Courthouse that Mace told Judge Frederici, "Now, judge, I took a lot from this woman for a long time. I stood for her old grandpappy lickin' the 'lasses pitcher for years, but when she cooked that polecat for supper the other night, saying it was cottontail rabbit, that was just too much." Judge Frederici granted the divorce.

Mace chauffeured for Doc Martin, who didn't care about the art of driving. They would go out to the dances where there had been gunfights. "Doc Martin's only tools," says Mace, "were a bottle of iodine and a pocket knife. He would run an iodine-soaked rag through the bullet hole, and the wounded man would generally live."

The only dentist in the country, and the first one to arrive, was Doc Muller. He pulled teeth with a pair of pliers at a dollar a tooth, and got rich at it.

MacHorse brought his cars over from Raton. They had to be pulled a lot of the way by mules. Finally a bunch of car-driving business men from Denver made it to Taos over the pass. Mace MacHorse, Doc Muller, and John were standing on the plaza looking over the model T's when John said, "Which one would you like to have, Doc?"

Muller picked a red one. That night John and the business men engaged in a little game of chance. The next morning John drove up in the car that Doc Muller had picked out, and gave it to him. He explained, "My luck was running last night, Doc."

Being the first automobile owner in Taos, it was only natural that John and his Ford created quite a little excitement. John had decided that sooner or later he would be forced to change to the automobile anyway. MacHorse says, "Because of the steep mountain roads, John ordered brake lining by the hundred foot roll.

When starting down a steep grade old John would make his customers get out and push *up* so as to save his brakes."

The roads were murderous on equipment. Those on John's stage route were made for horse-drawn transportation and, as mentioned before, people in those days built their own roads as they came to them. Being so destructively hard on cars, John soon learned to take care of them, and developed into quite a mechanic. He even discarded his old Stetson for one of the fashionable driving caps of the day. To tell the truth it was a long time before either his passengers or John himself felt any safer winding up out of the Rio Grande Gorge in an auto than they had in a stagecoach.

As time went on, and progress right along with it, highways were graded through to Taos from Santa Fe and Raton. Of course, this put John out of the stagecoach business altogether. He resented the coming of the mechanical age deeply, right to the last. It not only changed people's economics and methods of doing business, but it changed their personalities, too. They no longer needed to depend on their nearest neighbor for company, sympathy and entertainment. They could jump in the mechanical contraption, and in a short time be anywhere in the country—at a ball game, picture show, or any of the entertainments offered by the commercial world. John firmly believed the automobile did more to break up good solid friendships than anything else on earth. The reason, of course, was release from dependence on one another.

He realized the auto was here to stay, and if he sounded bitter about it, that's exactly the way he felt.

The most obvious change in Taos has taken place on the plaza. In the days when John first came to Taos, wagons, teams and saddle horses stood tied. Now automobiles are everywhere. Cars from every state in the Union can be seen at one time or another.

Tourists walk in throngs up and down the portal-covered sidewalks, shopping in the Indian and Mexican curio stores. There you can see Texas oil men in big brimmed hats, farmers from Kansas, business men from Denver, and people from all over the world, of every occupation. Mixed with the sightseers are Indians in blankets, Spanish farmers, sheep men, European notables, and, just as likely, Hollywood stars.

The results of John's belief and dream of Taos become more and more evident when the art galleries are visited. Paintings are on view by world-famous artists and the works of artists who want to be that way.

The small Spanish kids run up and say, "Shine, Sir, only ten cents." On Thursdays these same kids carry the *El Crepusculo* around and around the plaza yelling, "Paper, sir. Paper, sir." *The El Creeps,* as the paper is called by Taosensos, was the first paper ever published in New Mexico. It probably has the widest readership, for population, of any weekly paper in America. Its contents, edited by Lee Farran, range from art news and agriculture, to plain old everyday happenings.

Inside the *El Creeps* there is a one-sheet newspaper called *The Horse Fly*. It is subtitled, "The Smallest and Most Inadequate Newspaper in the World." It is a paper within a paper, and here may be found print that varies from intellectual poems to book reviews, or maybe an editorial sharply needling some Taos citizen. A fellow by the name of Spud Johnson ably edits this page. He has a number of avid followers, who wouldn't miss an issue for anything.

The lead story in the very first *Horse Fly*, announced: "TAOS SANTA CLAUS QUITS AFTER THIRTY-SIX YEARS," and was a tribute to John Dunn, "the Santa Claus who has brought Taos its Christmas presents, toys, candy, baubles, tourists, artists, love-letters and Monkey-Ward catalogues for thirty-six years. This hard-working St. Nicholas, without benefit of reindeer, carried passengers into Taos from 1902 until 1928; he carried the U. S. Mails, uninterruptedly, from 1906 to 1938. Last week he quit." And the *Horse Fly* sagely concluded: "If that isn't news, there ain't any."

In the summer, Taos holds two fiestas. The plaza is roped off, and no cars are allowed on it. Everyone goes, from the prospector in the hills to the retired merchant. They all wear the colorful fiesta costumes of the Southwest. There is music and dancing by both the Spanish and the Indians.

Jack Denver, Taos motel operator, runs a horse-drawn stagecoach to the pueblo and back each day. In the summer of 1952, John Dunn once again took the reins, and drove the stagecoach around the plaza, leading the parade. He received a big hand.

Taos has a calf-roping club that includes some members in odd professions indeed for calf-ropers. The president of the club is a dairyman, another a mechanic, and the list goes on like this: Telephone company manager, insurance salesman, lawyer, artist, writer, jukebox operator, tailor, theater operator, cafe man and, to save the day, a couple of ranchers and a cowboy.

Taos night life at times would do more than justice to the Paris left-bank. In its many cocktail lounges one may find winos, homosexuals (both sexes), artists of every description—from those who wear beards and paint one-eyed monsters, to those with the eye to realism. Some are starved, some only half-starved, and a few actually make a living at painting. The people in these places are friendly, and at the drop of a hat, or the purchase of a drink, will dance, sing or talk about the French moderns. A conversation in Taos can be struck up on anything.

It is a thing of beauty to see three cultures living together in such harmony. Except for the telephone, the electric light and the automobile, both the Indian and

Spanish live much as they did one hundred years ago. In the summer they work their little fields and gardens. They dry the corn, meat, beans and chile for the winter ahead. They get their firewood in early, in contrast to the Anglo who waits to the last minute or until the ground is already white with snow.

Little churches are scattered all over Taos Valley, and on Sunday afternoon the youngsters gather on the plaza to flirt and parade about in their best finery.

The Indians are constantly deluged with visitors at their thousand-year-old pueblo. When they have their corn dances and other ceremonials huge crowds gather.

A wedding in Taos is always heard, as well as seen. The Spanish on these occasions decorate their cars in long streamers of crepe paper, and drive around and around the plaza, blowing the car horns as loudly as possible. That night they always give a wedding dance, which is attended by scores of friends and relatives.

Today, up and down the streets of Taos, are many of John's old-time friends. Ruth Swaine, who for thirty years has rented her apartments to the great and near-great, always has something to say about John. Mike Cunico, famous old bronc-rider, and Doughbelly Price, rodeo-hand, gambler and Lord knows what else, invariably have a story to tell about something Long John once pulled.

Doughbelly Price is a famous little pot-bellied, ex-bronc-rider. Although Dough was a damn' good rider in earlier days, his fame has come about through his ever-ready wit—the sign on his real estate office being one example. It reads: DOUGHBELLY'S CLIP-JOINT. In his way he's a lot like John, except that John grew up straight as a steel rod and Doughbelly—well, he just never grew much in any direction. But he is not afraid of anything, except maybe conforming to a pattern. Doughbelly is one of the few individuals of the old western "don't give a damn school" left. He writes a column for over twenty-five newspapers, and he says what he pleases. He also capitalizes words in the middle of a sentence, and puts periods where there should be quotation marks. He probably does this just to please himself, for he sure doesn't care what the next person thinks about it.

When John died quietly on May 21, 1953, the *El Crepusculo* gave two-thirds of the front page space to Long John Dunn, the only time the paper has done that in its history. Doughbelly wrote then of his old friend. Here it is—word for mispelled word . . .

"The only old timer of his kind has cashed in his chips. There was just one john Dunn. The mould that made John as I see it had reached the Pinnacle of perfection when he was made and in that acion they broke the mould.

"For he was truly A character, stage driver, cowboy and gambler and the gambling instinct seemed to be the strongest as he had gambled all over the country—

Nevada in the gold rush days, California and in Taos for fifty year. John dunn dident apologize for the way he lived; he bragged about it. In that respect his life was an open Book, subject to enspection by any one. He would tell you about the money he had stold and give you days and dates where you could verify the story if you cared to.

"But just dont condem John Dunn to quick for that. You show me an old timer of his day that didnt do the same thing and some worse if they had the guts that John had and hold high the banner of honesty. And nine times out of ten I can show you A man that is handling the truth with gloves on to keep from leaving fingerprints. There was no skeleton in the closet for John. He was just what he was and dident care what the world thought of it or him.

"The early part of his life was rough rocky and uphill, that you could see by talking to him. He never mentioned the old swimming hole, the log School house, the loving touch of a Mothers hand or any of the joys of childhood that so many, even in his day, could look back on in the declining years of life. In his day it was A survival of the fittest and the fact that John was hovering on the ninty year mark showed that he was no dummy. His younger life was spent at hard work, not the kind that brings happiness and joy but backbreaking kind that warps and deforms the mind of some. But all the while he was doing that kind of work his mind was reaching out to things yet to come.

"In early life he was caught in the web of criminal law and the State of Texas give him forty years in the State penetentary, and JOHn told me, in that drawling through-the-nose talk of his, that he give them back thirty-nine years three months and some few days with old 'Bule', the prison blood hound right behind him. For many years he was a fugitive from justice, A lone wolf taking what it took to keep soul and body together and defying the world to come and get it back. He and his kind made this great United States what it is today, maybe not legally speaking but what them old timers done would be way short of the legal standards of today. But considering the times and the invorinment they had made them do as they done and they should be honored not censored.

"John dunn had no education. What he knowed, and don't mistake What he knowed, and dont mistke that knowledge, was plenty, he learned from cattle and horses and natural observation. things that he had to learn from mother nature, the hardest most tolerant and yet the wisest teacher humanity ever had. You learned or you dident surevive the battle. I had that teacher and for that reason I know what I am talking about. John dunn defied laws and customs as if they dident exist and went his way letting time set the pace. never it seems planning only for the day at hand. Tomorrow was another day and there would be other things and other fields to conquer.

"John Dunn was at his best, I think behind A roulette wheel or a monte table, where you never got more than was coming you and if you didn't watch it was less. In later years when most men of his age would be complaining and resting at home, I have seen john dunn stand for ten hours at A roulette wheel and never look up, never asleep on the job, and never over-looking a chance to slip you a short stack of chips. If caught, he dident argue. "shore, shore," he would say, "you cant blame a man for trying." I was racking chips for him one night on the wheel and there was two women and one man of the high society type playing. The women started talking French. John listened A spell and then he opened up "I shore wish you would talk english while you are playing at me," he said. "Oh we are so sorry Mr. Dunn. Dont you talk French?"

" 'No I dont talk French. I talk four languages and speak them fluently, but I dont talk French.'

" 'Oh how wonderful. What languages do you talk?'

" 'Some english, Profanity through my nose and slang' That was A typical answer from john Dunn.

"He never bet all his chips in no one hand. He was stage driver and carried the mail as well as passengers into Taos for years, first in the horse days and then come right on down to automobiles and had the first one ever owned in Taos.

"The material that he was made of is no more. He would get home at night, eat his supper, go deal Monte or run a wheel till daylight shoe A horse and sleep the balance of the time till it was time to go again. Geting tired was out of his line of thought.

"John Dunn has been cheered and been jeered, been on the high pedastal of hope and down in the depths of despair. Neither seemed to upset him any. He went his slow shuffling way looking neither to the right or left, asking few favors and not giving to many. He was a character himself, but like millions that is spawned every year he was tucked back onto the breast of mother earth. and will be forgotten in A way in a Short time, and his going will not cause a ripple on the waves of time."

John lived through three phases of the West—the gun-fighting days, the cattle-working days, and the present modern West. That's a pretty complete coverage in anybody's language.

John had come a long way, and done a lot of things since he ran away from old man Dunchee's farm back in Texas, but the results of his faith in Taos as a resort and internationally known art center will live forever.

Old Taos town and its people were extra bad and extra good to John. There was no in-between. He suffered three fires—all were hand-set. The ashes hadn't cooled each time before he was at work rebuilding. In one fire, he lost a store building next to the plaza, that was really worth the money. The other two were his homes.

Somebody got the habit of stealing Long John's firewood. It kept up quite a while. He was such a busy man he didn't have time to catch them.

It just so happened that some of John's acquaintances had secured some blasting powder from up in Twining Canyon, where there was a gold mining boom. No doubt they meant to blast someone's money out of its container. They had asked John if he would mind hiding this powder for them for a few days. He told them he'd be glad to keep it, since he had a particular use for it, too.

John bored holes in some of the firewood, and stuffed the powder inside, then plugged the holes up with sawdust. Before he had a chance to inform his wife about the plan, he was called to Santa Fe to a political meeting.

Adelaide, innocent of the whole affair, dropped a stick into the cook stove. Luckily, she walked into the other room, for about one second later the whole side of the house where the stove once stood was exposed to the elements by the blast. That was a hell of a fine joke on John, but it was all right with him. He'd pulled some good jokes on other people.

"One of the happiest days of my life," John once stated proudly, "was a few years back when the governor of the State of New Mexico delivered in person to me a full and free pardon from the State of Texas for my discrepancies therein."

Long John owned a big ten-room house right next to the plaza. It's a block up Governor Bent Street from the colorful Taos Inn. Bert Phillips, the pioneer artist, lived on the same street, and right across the street lives Becky James, another noted artist who paints on glass. She also does extraordinary embroidery.

The Dunn house is made of adobe, hard plastered, and built as strong as a fortress. It sits in the middle of one acre of good ground, and not a weed on the whole damned acre. Adelaide is responsible for the missing weeds and she didn't hire it done, either. John once remarked about this, "How in the hell she can take care of that house and land the way she does beats me. The house is always clean as can be, and yet she seems to have plenty of time left to scatter about town and get in lots of visiting."

John owned a biting dog that was so mean John didn't see how it ever lived as long as it had. When the dog was twelve years old he would bite anything that moved but John. It seems like he was just trying to look after John, for he never trained him to be that way.

There is one thing John said about the making of the West, and he had a right to say it: "Transportation made the West, not blazing guns as is so often preached —although I know the guns played a big part. It was those sweat-stained horses and tireless mules, those worn saddles and creaking wagons, and the men and women who were riding them across muddy rivers, rocky ridges and up those long dusty trails."

Whenever Long John felt a little restless he would walk up around the old Taos plaza and watch, as he so aptly put it, "the damned fool world that runs on rubber," and he added, "I hope to hell I can get past that biting dog of mine when I head back home."

EPILOGUE

In the last month of Nineteen Hundred and Fifty Two, when John was still ninety-four years old, he was struck down by an illness of the kidneys. He was rushed to the hospital. For days his urine was almost coal black. Everyone gave him up for gone. His children were notified.

What went through John's mind while he lay there in those white sheets only he will ever know. One thing is for sure, he had plenty to look back on. Most elderly people of his age would probably have been satisfied with that and passed on. John didn't.

In ten days he was back on his feet. In a few more he was home, but he didn't stay. He must have sensed that he had only a few traveling days left in this world.

First he went to his old-time and best friend, Mace MacHorse and said, "Mac, I want you to come over to the house and dig up some money for me."

MacHorse didn't question this, but asked, "Where is it?"

"It's in the basement, under the house."

"All right, let's go," agreed Mace.

John's wife was out visiting and he wanted to get the money and be gone before she got back.

MacHorse started digging where John pointed out. They both became absorbed in the interesting work of digging up money. MacHorse struck metal with the shovel and extracted the can of cash John had stashed away years before. They counted it—seventy five hundred dollars. Just as John had said.

MacHorse, driving a new Pontiac, which was a far cry from the Model T he had first sold John, took to the road. He and John went to Eagle Nest first, and then on over to E-Town, where John first stopped in New Mexico, and then wound their way through the mountains and valleys to Red River, the town John once had owned, and on over to the Rio Grande Gorge, where John had built the bridge of his dreams.

John got out and stood a minute and said, "It shore was hard, but it shore was fun." And the gears ground, and for the last time John pulled up his old stagecoach trail.

MacHorse took him over to Albuquerque to live with a young gambler friend that John once staked. In a short time, like an old dog that knows he's going to die, John headed home. It was his final trip. On May 22, 1953, the last breath left his body.

The old stagecoach trail is marked heavy from rubber tires. There is only about four square feet left of the wall of his "road-ranch" at the Rio Grande crossing, but if you listen on a still moonlight night you can hear the clatter of hard-running hoofs, the click of the dice, the whirl of the roulette wheel, and a tall man laughing shrilly through his nose.

WESTERNLORE PRESS

WESTERNLORE GREAT WEST AND INDIAN SERIES

Evans, Max.
     Long John Dunn of Taos.   Los Angeles, West-
ernlore Press, 1959.
     174p. illus. 22cm.   (Great West and Indian
series, 15)

207657

1.Dunn, John, 1857-1953. 2.Taos, N.M. 3.Frontier and
pioneer life-Southwest, New. I.Series.